The Big Book of Self-Analysis

Discover Your Untapped Potential

The Big Book of Self-Analysis: Discover Your Untapped Potential

For additional copies/bulk purchases of this book in the U.S. or internationally, please contact us at www.ericks.org

ISBN: 978-80-87518-12-0

Manufactured in the United States of America.

The Big Book of Self-Analysis

Discover Your Untapped Potential

Erickson Institute

Content

Establish Your Life's Timeline

Using your past experiences, categorize your life into seven distinct time frames. For example, if you're 40 years old, epoch 1 corresponds to ages 0 to 6, epoch 2 corresponds to ages 7 to 13, and so on. Consider dividing it into five epochs instead of seven if you're in your early twenties.

Epoch 1	
Epoch 2	
Epoch 3	
Epoch 4	
Epoch 5	
Epoch 6	
Epoch 7	

Epoch 1

Describe in detail three to seven significant events that occurred in your life during this time period. You can talk about the good and bad things that have happened to you. Each time period should include at least three significant events. Each experience should have a title and a short summary.

Epoch Experience 1A:

Label:

Description:

Effects: Describe the impact this event has had on your life and the person you have become as a result (write freely):

Epoch Experience 1B:

Label:

Description:

Effects: Describe the impact this event has had on your life and the person you have become as a result (write freely):

Epoch Experience 1C:

Label:

Description:

Effects: Describe the impact this event has had on your life and the person you have become as a result (write freely):

Epoch Experience 1D:

Label:

Description:

Effects: Describe the impact this event has had on your life and the person you have become as a result (write freely):

Epoch Experience 1E:

Label:

Description:

Effects: Describe the impact this event has had on your life and the person you have become as a result (write freely):

Epoch Experience 1F:

Label:

Description:

Effects: Describe the impact this event has had on your life and the person you have become as a result (write freely):

Epoch Experience 1G:

Label:

Description:

Effects: Describe the impact this event has had on your life and the person you have become as a result (write freely):

Epoch 2

Describe in detail three to seven significant events that occurred in your life during this time period. You can talk about the good and bad things that have happened to you. Each time period should include at least three significant events. Each experience should have a title and a short summary.

Epoch Experience 2A:

Label:

Description:

Effects: Describe the impact this event has had on your life and the person you have become as a result (write freely):

Epoch Experience 2B:

Label:

Description:

Effects: Describe the impact this event has had on your life and the person you have become as a result (write freely):

Epoch Experience 2C:

Label:

Description:

Effects: Describe the impact this event has had on your life and the person you have become as a result (write freely):

Epoch Experience 2D:

Label:

Description:

Effects: Describe the impact this event has had on your life and the person you have become as a result (write freely):

Epoch Experience 2E:

Label:

Description:

Effects: Describe the impact this event has had on your life and the person you have become as a result (write freely):

Epoch Experience 2F:

Label:

Description:

Effects: Describe the impact this event has had on your life and the person you have become as a result (write freely):

Epoch Experience 2G:

Label:

Description:

Effects: Describe the impact this event has had on your life and the person you have become as a result (write freely):

Epoch 3

Describe in detail three to seven significant events that occurred in your life during this time period. You can talk about the good and bad things that have happened to you. Each time period should include at least three significant events. Each experience should have a title and a short summary.

Epoch Experience 3A:

Label:

Description:

Effects: Describe the impact this event has had on your life and the person you have become as a result (write freely):

Epoch Experience 3B:

Label:

Description:

Effects: Describe the impact this event has had on your life and the person you have become as a result (write freely):

Epoch Experience 3C:

Label:

Description:

Effects: Describe the impact this event has had on your life and the person you have become as a result (write freely):

Epoch Experience 3D:

Label:

Description:

Effects: Describe the impact this event has had on your life and the person you have become as a result (write freely):

Epoch Experience 3E:

Label:

Description:

Effects: Describe the impact this event has had on your life and the person you have become as a result (write freely):

Epoch Experience 3F:

Label:

Description:

Effects: Describe the impact this event has had on your life and the person you have become as a result (write freely):

Epoch Experience 3G:

Label:

Description:

Effects: Describe the impact this event has had on your life and the person you have become as a result (write freely):

Epoch 4

Describe in detail three to seven significant events that occurred in your life during this time period. You can talk about the good and bad things that have happened to you. Each time period should include at least three significant events. Each experience should have a title and a short summary.

Epoch Experience 4A:

Label:

Description:

Effects: Describe the impact this event has had on your life and the person you have become as a result (write freely):

Epoch Experience 4B:

Label:

Description:

Effects: Describe the impact this event has had on your life and the person you have become as a result (write freely):

Epoch Experience 4C:

Label:

Description:

Effects: Describe the impact this event has had on your life and the person you have become as a result (write freely):

Epoch Experience 4D:

Label:

Description:

Effects: Describe the impact this event has had on your life and the person you have become as a result (write freely):

Epoch Experience 4E:

Label:

Description:

Effects: Describe the impact this event has had on your life and the person you have become as a result (write freely):

Epoch Experience 4F:

Label:

Description:

Effects: Describe the impact this event has had on your life and the person you have become as a result (write freely):

Epoch Experience 4G:

Label:

Description:

Effects: Describe the impact this event has had on your life and the person you have become as a result (write freely):

Epoch 5

Describe in detail three to seven significant events that occurred in your life during this time period. You can talk about the good and bad things that have happened to you. Each time period should include at least three significant events. Each experience should have a title and a short summary.

Epoch Experience 5A:

Label:

Description:

Effects: Describe the impact this event has had on your life and the person you have become as a result (write freely):

Epoch Experience 5B:

Label:

Description:

Effects: Describe the impact this event has had on your life and the person you have become as a result (write freely):

Epoch Experience 5C:

Label:

Description:

Effects: Describe the impact this event has had on your life and the person you have become as a result (write freely):

Epoch Experience 5D:

Label:

Description:

Effects: Describe the impact this event has had on your life and the person you have become as a result (write freely):

Epoch Experience 5E:

Label:

Description:

Effects: Describe the impact this event has had on your life and the person you have become as a result (write freely):

Epoch Experience 5F:

Label:

Description:

Effects: Describe the impact this event has had on your life and the person you have become as a result (write freely):

Epoch Experience 5G:

Label:

Description:

Effects: Describe the impact this event has had on your life and the person you have become as a result (write freely):

Epoch 6

Describe in detail three to seven significant events that occurred in your life during this time period. You can talk about the good and bad things that have happened to you. Each time period should include at least three significant events. Each experience should have a title and a short summary.

Epoch Experience 6A:

Label:

Description:

Effects: Describe the impact this event has had on your life and the person you have become as a result (write freely):

Epoch Experience 6B:

Label:

Description:

Effects: Describe the impact this event has had on your life and the person you have become as a result (write freely):

Epoch Experience 6C:

Label:

Description:

Effects: Describe the impact this event has had on your life and the person you have become as a result (write freely):

Epoch Experience 6D:

Label:

Description:

Effects: Describe the impact this event has had on your life and the person you have become as a result (write freely):

Epoch Experience 6E:

Label:

Description:

Effects: Describe the impact this event has had on your life and the person you have become as a result (write freely):

Epoch Experience 6F:

Label:

Description:

Effects: Describe the impact this event has had on your life and the person you have become as a result (write freely):

Epoch Experience 6G:

Label:

Description:

Effects: Describe the impact this event has had on your life and the person you have become as a result (write freely):

Epoch 7

Describe in detail three to seven significant events that occurred in your life during this time period. You can talk about the good and bad things that have happened to you. Each time period should include at least three significant events. Each experience should have a title and a short summary.

Epoch Experience 7A:

Label:

Description:

Effects: Describe the impact this event has had on your life and the person you have become as a result (write freely):

Epoch Experience 7B:

Label:

Description:

Effects: Describe the impact this event has had on your life and the person you have become as a result (write freely):

Epoch Experience 7C:

Label:

Description:

Effects: Describe the impact this event has had on your life and the person you have become as a result (write freely):

Epoch Experience 7D:

Label:

Description:

Effects: Describe the impact this event has had on your life and the person you have become as a result (write freely):

Epoch Experience 7E:

Label:

Description:

Effects: Describe the impact this event has had on your life and the person you have become as a result (write freely):

Epoch Experience 7F:

Label:

Description:

Effects: Describe the impact this event has had on your life and the person you have become as a result (write freely):

Epoch Experience 7G:

Label:

Description:

Effects: Describe the impact this event has had on your life and the person you have become as a result (write freely):

Summary Epoch 1

	Label
A	
B	
C	
D	
E	
F	
G	

Summary Epoch 2

	Label
A	
B	
C	
D	
E	
F	
G	

Summary Epoch 3

	Label
A	
B	
C	
D	
E	
F	
G	

Summary Epoch 4

	Label
A	
B	
C	
D	
E	
F	
G	

Summary Epoch 5

	Label
A	
B	
C	
D	
E	
F	
G	

Summary Epoch 6

	Label
A	
B	
C	
D	
E	
F	
G	

Summary Epoch 7

	Label
A	
B	
C	
D	
E	
F	
G	

Most Impactful Experiences

Identify the seven events that have had the greatest impact on your life. The significance of each of these will be explored in greater detail so that you can make sense of it all.

MIE	Epoch	Experience
1		
2		
3		
4		
5		
6		
7		

Most Impactful Experience 1

Label:

Write down the immediate thoughts and associations that come to your mind:

What happened to cause this experience?

Was it mostly positive or mostly negative?

How have other people supported or harmed you?

What part did you play in influencing the chain of events leading to this encounter during this time period?

Was there anything you could have handled differently?

Were there powerful factors that were beyond your control or grasp at the time?

What impact did this have on your faith in people?

What are your hopes and expectations?

What impact could changing it have on how much you value yourself and what life has to offer?

Your Answers:

Most Impactful Experience 2

Label:

Write down the immediate thoughts and associations that come to your mind:

What happened to cause this experience?

Was it mostly positive or mostly negative?

How have other people supported or harmed you?

What part did you play in influencing the chain of events leading to this encounter during this time period?

Was there anything you could have handled differently?

Were there powerful factors that were beyond your control or grasp at the time?

What impact did this have on your faith in people?

What are your hopes and expectations?

What impact could changing it have on how much you value yourself and what life has to offer?

Your Answers:

Most Impactful Experience 3

Label:

Write down the immediate thoughts and associations that come to your mind:

What happened to cause this experience?

Was it mostly positive or mostly negative?

How have other people supported or harmed you?

What part did you play in influencing the chain of events leading to this encounter during this time period?

Was there anything you could have handled differently?

Were there powerful factors that were beyond your control or grasp at the time?

What impact did this have on your faith in people?

What are your hopes and expectations?

What impact could changing it have on how much you value yourself and what life has to offer?

Your Answers:

Most Impactful Experience 4

Label:

Write down the immediate thoughts and associations that come to your mind:

What happened to cause this experience?

Was it mostly positive or mostly negative?

How have other people supported or harmed you?

What part did you play in influencing the chain of events leading to this encounter during this time period?

Was there anything you could have handled differently?

Were there powerful factors that were beyond your control or grasp at the time?

What impact did this have on your faith in people?

What are your hopes and expectations?

What impact could changing it have on how much you value yourself and what life has to offer?

Your Answers:

Most Impactful Experience 5

Label:

Write down the immediate thoughts and associations that come to your mind:

What happened to cause this experience?

Was it mostly positive or mostly negative?

How have other people supported or harmed you?

What part did you play in influencing the chain of events leading to this encounter during this time period?

Was there anything you could have handled differently?

Were there powerful factors that were beyond your control or grasp at the time?

What impact did this have on your faith in people?

What are your hopes and expectations?

What impact could changing it have on how much you value yourself and what life has to offer?

Your Answers:

Most Impactful Experience 6

Label:

Write down the immediate thoughts and associations that come to your mind:

What happened to cause this experience?

Was it mostly positive or mostly negative?

How have other people supported or harmed you?

What part did you play in influencing the chain of events leading to this encounter during this time period?

Was there anything you could have handled differently?

Were there powerful factors that were beyond your control or grasp at the time?

What impact did this have on your faith in people?

What are your hopes and expectations?

What impact could changing it have on how much you value yourself and what life has to offer?

Your Answers:

Most Impactful Experience 7

Label:

Write down the immediate thoughts and associations that come to your mind:

What happened to cause this experience?

Was it mostly positive or mostly negative?

How have other people supported or harmed you?

What part did you play in influencing the chain of events leading to this encounter during this time period?

Was there anything you could have handled differently?

Were there powerful factors that were beyond your control or grasp at the time?

What impact did this have on your faith in people?

What are your hopes and expectations?

What impact could changing it have on how much you value yourself and what life has to offer?

Your Answers:

Identify Your Core Beliefs

A person's core beliefs are the underlying presuppositions about themselves and the world they live in. Every aspect of your life, from your self-perception to your future goals to your moral compass, is influenced by your core beliefs. Despite the fact that you may occasionally be aware of your underlying beliefs, they often manifest themselves in an unconscious sort of way in your behavior.

Some fundamental beliefs are universal, such as the belief that corruption is inappropriate. As individuals and as a society, we all benefit from having these kinds of beliefs. Nevertheless, some fundamental beliefs can be limiting, especially if they promote a low opinion of yourself. Identifying your core beliefs, especially limiting ones, can help you enhance your behavior in a way that enables you to realize your full potential.

Your brain is constantly assessing the level of threat in your immediate surroundings. People's minds and bodies react to negative things happening to them by considering the surrounding environment as dangerous and preparing for remedial action. It is physically and emotionally draining to go through this process.

Your mind cannot rest until you've discovered a way to avoid experiencing the same pain and suffering again in the future if something awful happened to you in the past. By recalling various significant incidents from the past, you can assess how effectively you have handled this.

An inability to let go of the burden of the past is an indication that your mind isn't at rest and that you're still carrying it about with you, even though the memories in question are over a year and a half old.

As a result of unresolved conflicts from the past, you feel as if you are constantly at risk. You may feel wrath or dread and emotional anguish as a result of your body's response to stress under these situations. Chronic preparation might have negative effects on your emotional and physical well-being. A stress hormone called cortisol is released in greater quantities when you are in distress. However, your body uses your future reserves as fuel for action while you're in a crisis. You can't think clearly, your immune system is weakened, your energy is depleted, and the brain areas important for memory and emotional regulation are damaged by cortisol. Because of this, it is critical to maintain a stress level that is within reason.

The term "core beliefs" refers to deeply held convictions about oneself, others, the world, and one's place within it. Generally speaking, they can take the form of statements such as these:

"Most people are good."

It's difficult to get married.

"I don't have the skills necessary to do that."

And as you get older, especially in your teens and early twenties, you begin to form different core beliefs depending on your own life experience. Beneficial, neutral, or negative core beliefs are all possible. Their meaning depends on how you and others feel about them and how much they help or hinder your ability to function in the real world.

"In essence, people are decent."

"I could very well succeed if I put in the effort."

"I accept myself as I am."

Compare these with:

"No one likes me."

"Human beings are fundamentally selfish."

"If I fall in love with someone, they will abandon me."

Your core beliefs, which are based on your memories of the traumatic events that triggered these thoughts, must be exposed in order for you to take control of them. In the grand scheme of things, what happened to you was a long time ago. All that's left are the unconsciously formed neural connections between different stimuli and the negative emotions they elicit. Your current distress is caused by your negative core beliefs. Exposing them is akin to peering behind the curtain at the Wizard of Oz; it's not nearly as impressive in the light.

The way you perceive the world is heavily influenced by your core beliefs. They have a significant impact on the way you think, how you interpret the world, and how you make decisions. This is why it's a good idea to get to know your core beliefs.

People commonly hold a variety of both favourable and unfavourable beliefs about themselves. The following is a list of many beliefs that people may hold to differing degrees. Please rate how much you believe each statement truly depicts how you normally feel about yourself. Every now and then, open the book to a random page and choose a phrase.

Does it have the ring of authenticity about it?

Does it elicit new ideas, specific memories, regrets, desires, or even seemingly unrelated thoughts?

You may wish to explore these new insights and realizations with your therapist, or for self-therapy, apply any number of belief change protocols, such as those detailed in the new edition of The Big Book of NLP, Expanded.

1=Strongly Disbelieve; 2=Moderately Disbelieve; 3=Slightly Disbelieve; 4=Neutral; 5=Slightly Believe; 6=Moderately Believe; 7=Strongly Believe.

I abuse people's confidences.	1 | 2 | 3 | 4 | 5 | 6 | 7
I am told that I am a strong but fair leader.	1 | 2 | 3 | 4 | 5 | 6 | 7
I don't have a soft side.	1 | 2 | 3 | 4 | 5 | 6 | 7
I do not have a good imagination.	1 | 2 | 3 | 4 | 5 | 6 | 7
I am unsure about questions concerning politics, religion, or morality.	1 | 2 | 3 | 4 | 5 | 6 | 7
I don't have much energy.	1 | 2 | 3 | 4 | 5 | 6 | 7
I have little confidence in my decisions.	1 | 2 | 3 | 4 | 5 | 6 | 7
I am not highly motivated to succeed.	1 | 2 | 3 | 4 | 5 | 6 | 7
I don't have a place I call home.	1 | 2 | 3 | 4 | 5 | 6 | 7
I don't have strong feelings about anyone or anything.	1 | 2 | 3 | 4 | 5 | 6 | 7

I am unwilling to accept apologies.	1 | 2 | 3 | 4 | 5 | 6 | 7
I excel in nothing at all.	1 | 2 | 3 | 4 | 5 | 6 | 7
I am told that things I say are not polite.	1 | 2 | 3 | 4 | 5 | 6 | 7
I am only kind to others if they have been kind to me.	1 | 2 | 3 | 4 | 5 | 6 | 7
I am indifferent to the feelings of others.	1 | 2 | 3 | 4 | 5 | 6 | 7
I am a brave person.	1 | 2 | 3 | 4 | 5 | 6 | 7
I am an energetic person.	1 | 2 | 3 | 4 | 5 | 6 | 7
I am a lonely person.	1 | 2 | 3 | 4 | 5 | 6 | 7
I am a very reliable person.	1 | 2 | 3 | 4 | 5 | 6 | 7
I am a very private person.	1 | 2 | 3 | 4 | 5 | 6 | 7
I am a corrupt person.	1 | 2 | 3 | 4 | 5 | 6 | 7

I am a manipulative person.	1 | 2 | 3 | 4 | 5 | 6 | 7
I am a bitter person.	1 | 2 | 3 | 4 | 5 | 6 | 7
I am an extremely loyal person.	1 | 2 | 3 | 4 | 5 | 6 | 7
I am a vindictive person.	1 | 2 | 3 | 4 | 5 | 6 | 7
I am a sadistic person.	1 | 2 | 3 | 4 | 5 | 6 | 7
I am a cranky person.	1 | 2 | 3 | 4 | 5 | 6 | 7
I am a pessimistic person.	1 | 2 | 3 | 4 | 5 | 6 | 7
I am a jealous person.	1 | 2 | 3 | 4 | 5 | 6 | 7
I am a cold-hearted person.	1 | 2 | 3 | 4 | 5 | 6 | 7
I am an ordinary person with ordinary skills and abilities.	1 | 2 | 3 | 4 | 5 | 6 | 7
I am a spiritual person.	1 | 2 | 3 | 4 | 5 | 6 | 7

I am a negative type of person.	1 | 2 | 3 | 4 | 5 | 6 | 7
I am a person whose moods go up and down easily.	1 | 2 | 3 | 4 | 5 | 6 | 7
I automatically take charge.	1 | 2 | 3 | 4 | 5 | 6 | 7
I say what I think and feel even if I know other people will disagree.	1 | 2 | 3 | 4 | 5 | 6 | 7
I say I'm sorry when someone bumps into me in a crowd.	1 | 2 | 3 | 4 | 5 | 6 | 7
I collect things that I don't need.	1 | 2 | 3 | 4 | 5 | 6 | 7
I collect things that no one else wants.	1 | 2 | 3 | 4 | 5 | 6 | 7
I am a law-abiding citizen.	1 | 2 | 3 | 4 | 5 | 6 | 7
I am sluggish much of the time.	1 | 2 | 3 | 4 | 5 | 6 | 7
I am a very good scam artist.	1 | 2 | 3 | 4 | 5 | 6 | 7
I will try anything once.	1 | 2 | 3 | 4 | 5 | 6 | 7

I feel thankful for what I have received in life.	1 | 2 | 3 | 4 | 5 | 6 | 7
I will do anything for money.	1 | 2 | 3 | 4 | 5 | 6 | 7
I will do almost anything to avoid being rejected.	1 | 2 | 3 | 4 | 5 | 6 | 7
I will do just about anything to please people.	1 | 2 | 3 | 4 | 5 | 6 | 7
I am never bored.	1 | 2 | 3 | 4 | 5 | 6 | 7
I am never too busy to help a friend.	1 | 2 | 3 | 4 | 5 | 6 | 7
I am a submissive person.	1 | 2 | 3 | 4 | 5 | 6 | 7
I generally am not interested in doing very much.	1 | 2 | 3 | 4 | 5 | 6 | 7
I don't usually enjoy listening to people tell stories about events that have happened in their lives.	1 | 2 | 3 | 4 | 5 | 6 | 7
I generally feel like there isn't anything interesting or fun to do.	1 | 2 | 3 | 4 | 5 | 6 | 7
I generally give preference to those activities that imply an immediate gain.	1 | 2 | 3 | 4 | 5 | 6 | 7

I am usually skeptical about the future.	1 | 2 | 3 | 4 | 5 | 6 | 7
I am usually right.	1 | 2 | 3 | 4 | 5 | 6 | 7
I consult the library or the I internet immediately if I want to know something.	1 | 2 | 3 | 4 | 5 | 6 | 7
I check on things more often than necessary.	1 | 2 | 3 | 4 | 5 | 6 | 7
I examine my motives constantly.	1 | 2 | 3 | 4 | 5 | 6 | 7
I choose the easy way.	1 | 2 | 3 | 4 | 5 | 6 | 7
I choose my words with care.	1 | 2 | 3 | 4 | 5 | 6 | 7
I cry during movies.	1 | 2 | 3 | 4 | 5 | 6 | 7
I cry easily.	1 | 2 | 3 | 4 | 5 | 6 | 7
I am certain that I am being talked about.	1 | 2 | 3 | 4 | 5 | 6 | 7
I am on good terms with nearly everyone.	1 | 2 | 3 | 4 | 5 | 6 | 7

I am a shy person	1 | 2 | 3 | 4 | 5 | 6 | 7
I am unpredictable--people never know what I am going to say.	1 | 2 | 3 | 4 | 5 | 6 | 7
I am in good physical condition.	1 | 2 | 3 | 4 | 5 | 6 | 7
I am considered well-off financially.	1 | 2 | 3 | 4 | 5 | 6 | 7
I am often in a bad mood.	1 | 2 | 3 | 4 | 5 | 6 | 7
I doubt that most politicians are corrupt.	1 | 2 | 3 | 4 | 5 | 6 | 7
I easily lose my train of thought.	1 | 2 | 3 | 4 | 5 | 6 | 7
I am a bully.	1 | 2 | 3 | 4 | 5 | 6 | 7
I worry too much about what others might think.	1 | 2 | 3 | 4 | 5 | 6 | 7
I demand quality.	1 | 2 | 3 | 4 | 5 | 6 | 7
I demand the impossible of others.	1 | 2 | 3 | 4 | 5 | 6 | 7

I demand explanations from others.	1 | 2 | 3 | 4 | 5 | 6 | 7
I demand a lot from others.	1 | 2 | 3 | 4 | 5 | 6 | 7
I demand to be the center of interest.	1 | 2 | 3 | 4 | 5 | 6 | 7
I demand obedience.	1 | 2 | 3 | 4 | 5 | 6 | 7
I demand perfection in others.	1 | 2 | 3 | 4 | 5 | 6 | 7
I demand attention.	1 | 2 | 3 | 4 | 5 | 6 | 7
I demand perfection in myself.	1 | 2 | 3 | 4 | 5 | 6 | 7
I am the most important person in someone else's life.	1 | 2 | 3 | 4 | 5 | 6 | 7
I am an original thinker.	1 | 2 | 3 | 4 | 5 | 6 | 7
I get lost in my dreams.	1 | 2 | 3 | 4 | 5 | 6 | 7
I can recall many events before the age of three.	1 | 2 | 3 | 4 | 5 | 6 | 7

I experience my emotions intensely.	1 | 2 | 3 | 4 | 5 | 6 | 7
I experience supernatural guidance.	1 | 2 | 3 | 4 | 5 | 6 | 7
I experience a lot of physical pain.	1 | 2 | 3 | 4 | 5 | 6 | 7
I experience panic spells.	1 | 2 | 3 | 4 | 5 | 6 | 7
I experience pangs of hunger that cause me to devour everything insight.	1 | 2 | 3 | 4 | 5 | 6 | 7
I experience very few emotional highs and lows.	1 | 2 | 3 | 4 | 5 | 6 | 7
I experience moods that bounce around like a pinball machine.	1 | 2 | 3 | 4 | 5 | 6 | 7
I experience altered states of consciousness.	1 | 2 | 3 | 4 | 5 | 6 | 7
I experience deep emotions when I see beautiful things.	1 | 2 | 3 | 4 | 5 | 6 | 7
I experience longer periods of sadness or depression than other people seem to.	1 | 2 | 3 | 4 | 5 | 6 | 7
I am generally fearful of bad things that could happen.	1 | 2 | 3 | 4 | 5 | 6 | 7

I fear for the worst.	1 | 2 | 3 | 4 | 5 | 6 | 7
I would be afraid to give a speech in public.	1 | 2 | 3 | 4 | 5 | 6 | 7
I fear that others will hate me.	1 | 2 | 3 | 4 | 5 | 6 | 7
I am without talent.	1 | 2 | 3 | 4 | 5 | 6 | 7
I am worthless.	1 | 2 | 3 | 4 | 5 | 6 | 7
I feel little concern for others.	1 | 2 | 3 | 4 | 5 | 6 | 7
I am bothered by frequent aches and pains.	1 | 2 | 3 | 4 | 5 | 6 | 7
I feel that nothing seems to make me feel good.	1 | 2 | 3 | 4 | 5 | 6 | 7
I feel that yelling helps me feel better.	1 | 2 | 3 | 4 | 5 | 6 | 7
I am good at making impromptu speeches.	1 | 2 | 3 | 4 | 5 | 6 | 7
I am good at many things.	1 | 2 | 3 | 4 | 5 | 6 | 7

I am good at making excuses for my bad behavior.	1 | 2 | 3 | 4 | 5 | 6 | 7
I am good at analyzing problems.	1 | 2 | 3 | 4 | 5 | 6 | 7
I claim to be able to do everything.	1 | 2 | 3 | 4 | 5 | 6 | 7
I admire a really clever scam.	1 | 2 | 3 | 4 | 5 | 6 | 7
I am good at using people's weak points to my advantage.	1 | 2 | 3 | 4 | 5 | 6 | 7
I create problems for others.	1 | 2 | 3 | 4 | 5 | 6 | 7
I make difficulties out of nothing.	1 | 2 | 3 | 4 | 5 | 6 | 7
I am more capable than most others.	1 | 2 | 3 | 4 | 5 | 6 | 7
I can improvise.	1 | 2 | 3 | 4 | 5 | 6 | 7
I can easily become furious.	1 | 2 | 3 | 4 | 5 | 6 | 7
I can spend hours doing nothing.	1 | 2 | 3 | 4 | 5 | 6 | 7

I can perform a wide variety of tasks.	1 | 2 | 3 | 4 | 5 | 6 | 7
I am able to get other people to act in a certain way.	1 | 2 | 3 | 4 | 5 | 6 | 7
I can make anyone believe anything I want them to.	1 | 2 | 3 | 4 | 5 | 6 | 7
I can make myself work on a difficult task even when I don't feel like trying.	1 | 2 | 3 | 4 | 5 | 6 | 7
I am able to see the best in a situation.	1 | 2 | 3 | 4 | 5 | 6 | 7
I can express love to someone else.	1 | 2 | 3 | 4 | 5 | 6 | 7
I can be very cruel to people.	1 | 2 | 3 | 4 | 5 | 6 | 7
I can get anxious, depressed, or irritable for no reason.	1 | 2 | 3 | 4 | 5 | 6 | 7
I can be vicious.	1 | 2 | 3 | 4 | 5 | 6 | 7
I can remain cool-headed when stressed out.	1 | 2 | 3 | 4 | 5 | 6 | 7
I am able to come up with new and different ideas.	1 | 2 | 3 | 4 | 5 | 6 | 7

I can get along with most people.	1 | 2 | 3 | 4 | 5 | 6 | 7
I am able to fit into any situation.	1 | 2 | 3 | 4 | 5 | 6 | 7
I can handle complex problems.	1 | 2 | 3 | 4 | 5 | 6 | 7
I can face my fears.	1 | 2 | 3 | 4 | 5 | 6 | 7
I can handle a lot of information.	1 | 2 | 3 | 4 | 5 | 6 | 7
I can spot faulty reasoning.	1 | 2 | 3 | 4 | 5 | 6 | 7
I can go from cheerful to furious, or vice versa, very quickly.	1 | 2 | 3 | 4 | 5 | 6 | 7
I can sense how things will turn out.	1 | 2 | 3 | 4 | 5 | 6 | 7
I can see into the future.	1 | 2 | 3 | 4 | 5 | 6 | 7
I can think of many different ways to solve problems.	1 | 2 | 3 | 4 | 5 | 6 | 7
I can think of one or more times in my life where I was very brave.	1 | 2 | 3 | 4 | 5 | 6 | 7

I can create any impression that I want.	1 | 2 | 3 | 4 | 5 | 6 | 7
I can find the positive in what seems negative to others.	1 | 2 | 3 | 4 | 5 | 6 | 7
I can find something of interest in any situation.	1 | 2 | 3 | 4 | 5 | 6 | 7
I can manage many things at the same time.	1 | 2 | 3 | 4 | 5 | 6 | 7
I can work under pressure.	1 | 2 | 3 | 4 | 5 | 6 | 7
I can stand a great deal of stress.	1 | 2 | 3 | 4 | 5 | 6 | 7
I can get out of difficult situations.	1 | 2 | 3 | 4 | 5 | 6 | 7
I can accept criticism without getting upset.	1 | 2 | 3 | 4 | 5 | 6 | 7
I can take the viewpoint of others.	1 | 2 | 3 | 4 | 5 | 6 | 7
I am able to read the minds of others.	1 | 2 | 3 | 4 | 5 | 6 | 7
I can read books written in I chinese.	1 | 2 | 3 | 4 | 5 | 6 | 7

I am able to see how other peoples' emotions can affect their behaviors.	1 | 2 | 3 | 4 | 5 | 6 | 7
I can see the funny side of a painful situation.	1 | 2 | 3 | 4 | 5 | 6 | 7
I can clearly picture in my mind what I want to happen in my future.	1 | 2 | 3 | 4 | 5 | 6 | 7
I can see different points of view.	1 | 2 | 3 | 4 | 5 | 6 | 7
I can see special connections between seemingly unrelated objects or events.	1 | 2 | 3 | 4 | 5 | 6 | 7
I can play many roles convincingly.	1 | 2 | 3 | 4 | 5 | 6 | 7
I can take my mind off my problems.	1 | 2 | 3 | 4 | 5 | 6 | 7
I can control objects with my mind.	1 | 2 | 3 | 4 | 5 | 6 | 7
I can control my emotions.	1 | 2 | 3 | 4 | 5 | 6 | 7
I can keep a secret.	1 | 2 | 3 | 4 | 5 | 6 | 7
I can stay on a diet.	1 | 2 | 3 | 4 | 5 | 6 | 7

I can change the weather simply by thinking about it.	1 | 2 | 3 | 4 | 5 | 6 | 7
I am able to describe my feelings easily.	1 | 2 | 3 | 4 | 5 | 6 | 7
I am a creature of habit.	1 | 2 | 3 | 4 | 5 | 6 | 7
I am a large-sized person.	1 | 2 | 3 | 4 | 5 | 6 | 7
I am angry or distressed when my partner pays more attention to someone else.	1 | 2 | 3 | 4 | 5 | 6 | 7
I am constantly reflecting about myself.	1 | 2 | 3 | 4 | 5 | 6 | 7
I am open about my feelings.	1 | 2 | 3 | 4 | 5 | 6 | 7
I am not a caring person.	1 | 2 | 3 | 4 | 5 | 6 | 7
I am not a joyful person.	1 | 2 | 3 | 4 | 5 | 6 | 7
I don't like crowded events.	1 | 2 | 3 | 4 | 5 | 6 | 7
I dislike myself.	1 | 2 | 3 | 4 | 5 | 6 | 7

I dislike surprises.	1 | 2 | 3 | 4 | 5 | 6 | 7
I do not enjoy going to art museums.	1 | 2 | 3 | 4 | 5 | 6 | 7
I dislike talking about myself.	1 | 2 | 3 | 4 | 5 | 6 | 7
I don't like to spend money.	1 | 2 | 3 | 4 | 5 | 6 | 7
I dislike being the center of attention.	1 | 2 | 3 | 4 | 5 | 6 | 7
I don't like being away from civilization.	1 | 2 | 3 | 4 | 5 | 6 | 7
I dislike being around happy people when I'm feeling sad.	1 | 2 | 3 | 4 | 5 | 6 | 7
I dislike looking at myself in the mirror.	1 | 2 | 3 | 4 | 5 | 6 | 7
I dislike competing with others.	1 | 2 | 3 | 4 | 5 | 6 | 7
I do not enjoy kissing.	1 | 2 | 3 | 4 | 5 | 6 | 7
I don't like to get involved in other people's problems.	1 | 2 | 3 | 4 | 5 | 6 | 7

I don't like to ponder over things.	1 | 2 | 3 | 4 | 5 | 6 | 7
I do not like concerts.	1 | 2 | 3 | 4 | 5 | 6 | 7
I don't like to learn new things.	1 | 2 | 3 | 4 | 5 | 6 | 7
I dislike learning.	1 | 2 | 3 | 4 | 5 | 6 | 7
I dislike new foods.	1 | 2 | 3 | 4 | 5 | 6 | 7
I dislike having to do more than one task at a time.	1 | 2 | 3 | 4 | 5 | 6 | 7
I don't like running errands for others.	1 | 2 | 3 | 4 | 5 | 6 | 7
I dislike being complimented.	1 | 2 | 3 | 4 | 5 | 6 | 7
I dislike taking responsibility for making decisions.	1 | 2 | 3 | 4 | 5 | 6 | 7
I do not like reading or hearing opinions that go against my way of thinking.	1 | 2 | 3 | 4 | 5 | 6 | 7
I don't like seeing people dressed carelessly.	1 | 2 | 3 | 4 | 5 | 6 | 7

I dislike loud music.	1 | 2 | 3 | 4 | 5 | 6 | 7
I don't like action movies.	1 | 2 | 3 | 4 | 5 | 6 | 7
I dislike changes.	1 | 2 | 3 | 4 | 5 | 6 | 7
I do not like poetry.	1 | 2 | 3 | 4 | 5 | 6 | 7
I don't like being interrupted.	1 | 2 | 3 | 4 | 5 | 6 | 7
I do not trust the integrity of the police.	1 | 2 | 3 | 4 | 5 | 6 | 7
I distrust the medical profession to handle my health.	1 | 2 | 3 | 4 | 5 | 6 | 7
I am not sure where my life is going.	1 | 2 | 3 | 4 | 5 | 6 | 7
I am physically out of shape.	1 | 2 | 3 | 4 | 5 | 6 | 7
I am not picky about food.	1 | 2 | 3 | 4 | 5 | 6 | 7
I don't pride myself on being original.	1 | 2 | 3 | 4 | 5 | 6 | 7

I don't worry about things that have already happened.	1 | 2 | 3 | 4 | 5 | 6 | 7
I can't remember the last time I thought about sex.	1 | 2 | 3 | 4 | 5 | 6 | 7
I can't remember the last time I smiled.	1 | 2 | 3 | 4 | 5 | 6 | 7
I do not easily share my feelings with others.	1 | 2 | 3 | 4 | 5 | 6 | 7
I don't think straight when I am upset.	1 | 2 | 3 | 4 | 5 | 6 | 7
I don't think much about sex.	1 | 2 | 3 | 4 | 5 | 6 | 7
I don't think as well as I used to.	1 | 2 | 3 | 4 | 5 | 6 | 7
I don't think about more possibilities than the one I like first.	1 | 2 | 3 | 4 | 5 | 6 | 7
I don't think about different possibilities when making decisions.	1 | 2 | 3 | 4 | 5 | 6 | 7
I do not think about decisions.	1 | 2 | 3 | 4 | 5 | 6 | 7
I don't think of tomorrow.	1 | 2 | 3 | 4 | 5 | 6 | 7

I don't think that I'm better than other people.	1 | 2 | 3 | 4 | 5 | 6 | 7
I don't think I should have to wait in lines like others.	1 | 2 | 3 | 4 | 5 | 6 | 7
I don't think that schooling is important.	1 | 2 | 3 | 4 | 5 | 6 | 7
I don't think that laws apply to me.	1 | 2 | 3 | 4 | 5 | 6 | 7
I don't think it's important to socialize with others.	1 | 2 | 3 | 4 | 5 | 6 | 7
I don't consider myself attractive.	1 | 2 | 3 | 4 | 5 | 6 | 7
I fear nothing.	1 | 2 | 3 | 4 | 5 | 6 | 7
I don't take orders well.	1 | 2 | 3 | 4 | 5 | 6 | 7
I am not good at taking charge of a group.	1 | 2 | 3 | 4 | 5 | 6 | 7
I am not good at deceiving other people.	1 | 2 | 3 | 4 | 5 | 6 | 7
I am not good at sports.	1 | 2 | 3 | 4 | 5 | 6 | 7

I am not good at working with a group.	1 | 2 | 3 | 4 | 5 | 6 | 7
I don't bother to make an effort.	1 | 2 | 3 | 4 | 5 | 6 | 7
I don't know how to handle myself in a new social situation.	1 | 2 | 3 | 4 | 5 | 6 | 7
I don't know much about history.	1 | 2 | 3 | 4 | 5 | 6 | 7
I don't know why I'm angry.	1 | 2 | 3 | 4 | 5 | 6 | 7
I don't know why I do some of the things I do.	1 | 2 | 3 | 4 | 5 | 6 | 7
I don't know what's going on inside me.	1 | 2 | 3 | 4 | 5 | 6 | 7
I could never imagine hurting another person.	1 | 2 | 3 | 4 | 5 | 6 | 7
I can't say no.	1 | 2 | 3 | 4 | 5 | 6 | 7
I can't be bothered with other's needs.	1 | 2 | 3 | 4 | 5 | 6 | 7
I can't do without the company of others.	1 | 2 | 3 | 4 | 5 | 6 | 7

I can't come up with new ideas.	1 | 2 | 3 | 4 | 5 | 6 | 7
I cannot stop thinking about all of my mistakes.	1 | 2 | 3 | 4 | 5 | 6 | 7
I can't afford to buy things I need.	1 | 2 | 3 | 4 | 5 | 6 | 7
I can't concentrate.	1 | 2 | 3 | 4 | 5 | 6 | 7
I can't stand waiting.	1 | 2 | 3 | 4 | 5 | 6 | 7
I can't think clearly when under pressure.	1 | 2 | 3 | 4 | 5 | 6 | 7
I can't put my ideas into practice.	1 | 2 | 3 | 4 | 5 | 6 | 7
I can't stand nosey people.	1 | 2 | 3 | 4 | 5 | 6 | 7
I can't stand weak people.	1 | 2 | 3 | 4 | 5 | 6 | 7
I can't stand impolite people.	1 | 2 | 3 | 4 | 5 | 6 | 7
I can't stand aggressive people.	1 | 2 | 3 | 4 | 5 | 6 | 7

I can't stand confrontations.	1 | 2 | 3 | 4 | 5 | 6 | 7
I cannot control the urge to hurt myself when something goes wrong.	1 | 2 | 3 | 4 | 5 | 6 | 7
I can't control my impulses when I'm really stressed.	1 | 2 | 3 | 4 | 5 | 6 | 7
I can never keep a secret.	1 | 2 | 3 | 4 | 5 | 6 | 7
I can't resist eating candy or cookies if they are around.	1 | 2 | 3 | 4 | 5 | 6 | 7
I don't wear fashionable clothing.	1 | 2 | 3 | 4 | 5 | 6 | 7
I don't learn from my experiences.	1 | 2 | 3 | 4 | 5 | 6 | 7
I do not take news at face value.	1 | 2 | 3 | 4 | 5 | 6 | 7
I do not take many risks.	1 | 2 | 3 | 4 | 5 | 6 | 7
I don't lose my head.	1 | 2 | 3 | 4 | 5 | 6 | 7
I do not believe in a universal power or a I god.	1 | 2 | 3 | 4 | 5 | 6 | 7

I do not believe humans are truly capable of love.	1 | 2 | 3 | 4 | 5 | 6 | 7
I don't waste time with others' troubles.	1 | 2 | 3 | 4 | 5 | 6 | 7
I don't get sidetracked when I work.	1 | 2 | 3 | 4 | 5 | 6 | 7
I don't understand people who get emotional.	1 | 2 | 3 | 4 | 5 | 6 | 7
I don't reveal my intentions.	1 | 2 | 3 | 4 | 5 | 6 | 7
I do not stand up for my beliefs.	1 | 2 | 3 | 4 | 5 | 6 | 7
I don't speak my mind freely when there might be negative results.	1 | 2 | 3 | 4 | 5 | 6 | 7
I don't talk a lot.	1 | 2 | 3 | 4 | 5 | 6 | 7
I don't hesitate to express an unpopular opinion.	1 | 2 | 3 | 4 | 5 | 6 | 7
I don't bother worrying about political and social problems.	1 | 2 | 3 | 4 | 5 | 6 | 7
I don't know what I really want.	1 | 2 | 3 | 4 | 5 | 6 | 7

I do not give up easily.	1 | 2 | 3 | 4 | 5 | 6 | 7
I don't discard old pictures or snapshots	1 | 2 | 3 | 4 | 5 | 6 | 7
I am not disturbed by events.	1 | 2 | 3 | 4 | 5 | 6 | 7
I am not bothered by disorder.	1 | 2 | 3 | 4 | 5 | 6 | 7
I am not bothered by crazy thoughts.	1 | 2 | 3 | 4 | 5 | 6 | 7
I can't find the right words for my feelings.	1 | 2 | 3 | 4 | 5 | 6 | 7
I am not easily affected by my emotions.	1 | 2 | 3 | 4 | 5 | 6 | 7
I am unaffected by the suffering of others.	1 | 2 | 3 | 4 | 5 | 6 | 7
I am not affected by either praise or criticism.	1 | 2 | 3 | 4 | 5 | 6 | 7
I am not in touch with my feelings.	1 | 2 | 3 | 4 | 5 | 6 | 7
I don't indulge in violence.	1 | 2 | 3 | 4 | 5 | 6 | 7

I do not make polite excuses.	1 | 2 | 3 | 4 | 5 | 6 | 7
I don't try to figure myself out.	1 | 2 | 3 | 4 | 5 | 6 | 7
I don't strive for elegance in my appearance.	1 | 2 | 3 | 4 | 5 | 6 | 7
I don't try to get even.	1 | 2 | 3 | 4 | 5 | 6 | 7
I don't analyze the reasons for my actions.	1 | 2 | 3 | 4 | 5 | 6 | 7
I can't stand being alone.	1 | 2 | 3 | 4 | 5 | 6 | 7
I am unable to do some of the things I would like to do because of my health.	1 | 2 | 3 | 4 | 5 | 6 | 7
I can't make up my mind.	1 | 2 | 3 | 4 | 5 | 6 | 7
I am unable to do things properly.	1 | 2 | 3 | 4 | 5 | 6 | 7
I am not happy until all the details are taken care of.	1 | 2 | 3 | 4 | 5 | 6 | 7
I don't finish what I start.	1 | 2 | 3 | 4 | 5 | 6 | 7

Statement	Rating
I am not good at hiding my intentions from others.	1 | 2 | 3 | 4 | 5 | 6 | 7
I am not interested in theoretical discussions.	1 | 2 | 3 | 4 | 5 | 6 | 7
I am not afraid of providing criticism.	1 | 2 | 3 | 4 | 5 | 6 | 7
I am not much of a flirt.	1 | 2 | 3 | 4 | 5 | 6 | 7
I am not good at getting people to like me.	1 | 2 | 3 | 4 | 5 | 6 | 7
I am not good at figuring out what really matters.	1 | 2 | 3 | 4 | 5 | 6 | 7
I cannot seem to deal with stress at work/school.	1 | 2 | 3 | 4 | 5 | 6 | 7
I don't pay much attention to the material objects other people own.	1 | 2 | 3 | 4 | 5 | 6 | 7
I don't show my feelings.	1 | 2 | 3 | 4 | 5 | 6 | 7
I do not often talk about things that I have achieved.	1 | 2 | 3 | 4 | 5 | 6 | 7
I don't feel the need to be close to others.	1 | 2 | 3 | 4 | 5 | 6 | 7

I do not feel close to people.	1 | 2 | 3 | 4 | 5 | 6 | 7
I feel no gratitude to others.	1 | 2 | 3 | 4 | 5 | 6 | 7
I don't soften the truth.	1 | 2 | 3 | 4 | 5 | 6 | 7
I don't let others discourage me.	1 | 2 | 3 | 4 | 5 | 6 | 7
I don't let others cut in front of me in line.	1 | 2 | 3 | 4 | 5 | 6 | 7
I do not go out of my way to make others smile or laugh.	1 | 2 | 3 | 4 | 5 | 6 | 7
I don't use harsh language.	1 | 2 | 3 | 4 | 5 | 6 | 7
I don't miss group meetings or team practices.	1 | 2 | 3 | 4 | 5 | 6 | 7
I don't commit myself to things.	1 | 2 | 3 | 4 | 5 | 6 | 7
I don't pretend to be more than I am.	1 | 2 | 3 | 4 | 5 | 6 | 7
I do not plan ahead.	1 | 2 | 3 | 4 | 5 | 6 | 7

I don't plan anything very far in advance.	1 | 2 | 3 | 4 | 5 | 6 | 7
I don't act like a show-off.	1 | 2 | 3 | 4 | 5 | 6 | 7
I don't act is if I'm a special person.	1 | 2 | 3 | 4 | 5 | 6 | 7
I do not exercise on a regular basis.	1 | 2 | 3 | 4 | 5 | 6 | 7
I am not interested in other people's problems.	1 | 2 | 3 | 4 | 5 | 6 | 7
I am not interested in romance.	1 | 2 | 3 | 4 | 5 | 6 | 7
I don't call people just to talk.	1 | 2 | 3 | 4 | 5 | 6 | 7
I don't brag about my accomplishments.	1 | 2 | 3 | 4 | 5 | 6 | 7
I don't get particularly upset when I lose things.	1 | 2 | 3 | 4 | 5 | 6 | 7
I am not easily annoyed.	1 | 2 | 3 | 4 | 5 | 6 | 7
I don't get excited about things.	1 | 2 | 3 | 4 | 5 | 6 | 7

I don't enjoy being in the spotlight.	1 | 2 | 3 | 4 | 5 | 6 | 7
I don't enjoy being the object of jokes.	1 | 2 | 3 | 4 | 5 | 6 | 7
I dislike looking at my body.	1 | 2 | 3 | 4 | 5 | 6 | 7
I don't like to travel.	1 | 2 | 3 | 4 | 5 | 6 | 7
I do not enjoy watching dance performances.	1 | 2 | 3 | 4 | 5 | 6 | 7
I don't like sex.	1 | 2 | 3 | 4 | 5 | 6 | 7
I don't enjoy doing quiet leisure activities.	1 | 2 | 3 | 4 | 5 | 6 | 7
I do not tend to stick with what I decide to do.	1 | 2 | 3 | 4 | 5 | 6 | 7
I don't tend to think things through critically.	1 | 2 | 3 | 4 | 5 | 6 | 7
I don't let others take credit for my work.	1 | 2 | 3 | 4 | 5 | 6 | 7
I do not give anyone a second chance to hurt me.	1 | 2 | 3 | 4 | 5 | 6 | 7

I don't let little things anger me.	1 | 2 | 3 | 4 | 5 | 6 | 7
I don't let an illness or injury change my daily habits.	1 | 2 | 3 | 4 | 5 | 6 | 7
I don't tolerate critics.	1 | 2 | 3 | 4 | 5 | 6 | 7
I dislike neon signs and florescent colors.	1 | 2 | 3 | 4 | 5 | 6 | 7
I distrust people.	1 | 2 | 3 | 4 | 5 | 6 | 7
I don't quit a task before it is finished.	1 | 2 | 3 | 4 | 5 | 6 | 7
I don't approach things halfheartedly.	1 | 2 | 3 | 4 | 5 | 6 | 7
I don't make a big deal about gifts that I receive.	1 | 2 | 3 | 4 | 5 | 6 | 7
I do not make lists.	1 | 2 | 3 | 4 | 5 | 6 | 7
I do not quit easily, even when things are hard.	1 | 2 | 3 | 4 | 5 | 6 | 7
I don't read nonfiction books for fun.	1 | 2 | 3 | 4 | 5 | 6 | 7

I am not as strict as I should be.	1 | 2 | 3 | 4 | 5 | 6 | 7
I don't consider myself religious.	1 | 2 | 3 | 4 | 5 | 6 | 7
I don't see much hope for myself.	1 | 2 | 3 | 4 | 5 | 6 | 7
I do not see the need to acknowledge others who are good to me.	1 | 2 | 3 | 4 | 5 | 6 | 7
I don't want to cause trouble.	1 | 2 | 3 | 4 | 5 | 6 | 7
I don't like to share, even when others desperately need what I have.	1 | 2 | 3 | 4 | 5 | 6 | 7
I don't desire things that others have.	1 | 2 | 3 | 4 | 5 | 6 | 7
I do not practice any religion.	1 | 2 | 3 | 4 | 5 | 6 | 7
I don't pay attention.	1 | 2 | 3 | 4 | 5 | 6 | 7
I don't pay enough attention when others are speaking to me.	1 | 2 | 3 | 4 | 5 | 6 | 7
I am not always honest with myself.	1 | 2 | 3 | 4 | 5 | 6 | 7

I don't always practice what I preach.	1 | 2 | 3 | 4 | 5 | 6 | 7
I acquire skills quickly.	1 | 2 | 3 | 4 | 5 | 6 | 7
I am not embarrassed easily.	1 | 2 | 3 | 4 | 5 | 6 | 7
I am sometimes full of thoughts, ideas, and images in my mind.	1 | 2 | 3 | 4 | 5 | 6 | 7
I easily lose track of reality.	1 | 2 | 3 | 4 | 5 | 6 | 7
I am very shy in social situations.	1 | 2 | 3 | 4 | 5 | 6 | 7
I am very insecure in my relationships.	1 | 2 | 3 | 4 | 5 | 6 | 7
I am very pleased with myself.	1 | 2 | 3 | 4 | 5 | 6 | 7
I am inexplicably happy some of the time.	1 | 2 | 3 | 4 | 5 | 6 | 7
I am guided by superstitions.	1 | 2 | 3 | 4 | 5 | 6 | 7
I believe in things that have no scientific explanation.	1 | 2 | 3 | 4 | 5 | 6 | 7

I believe in one true religion.	1 | 2 | 3 | 4 | 5 | 6 | 7
I believe in a life after death.	1 | 2 | 3 | 4 | 5 | 6 | 7
I believe in the importance of art.	1 | 2 | 3 | 4 | 5 | 6 | 7
I believe in the importance of tradition.	1 | 2 | 3 | 4 | 5 | 6 | 7
I believe in the power of astrology to predict the future.	1 | 2 | 3 | 4 | 5 | 6 | 7
I believe in the power of fate.	1 | 2 | 3 | 4 | 5 | 6 | 7
I believe in the power of tarot cards to predict the future.	1 | 2 | 3 | 4 | 5 | 6 | 7
I believe in an eye for an eye.	1 | 2 | 3 | 4 | 5 | 6 | 7
I believe in sexual modesty.	1 | 2 | 3 | 4 | 5 | 6 | 7
I believe in equality between all races.	1 | 2 | 3 | 4 | 5 | 6 | 7
I believe that one race of people is better than others.	1 | 2 | 3 | 4 | 5 | 6 | 7

I believe that our human nature brings us together to work for common goals.	1 | 2 | 3 | 4 | 5 | 6 | 7
I believe that good will always beat evil.	1 | 2 | 3 | 4 | 5 | 6 | 7
I believe that the world is controlled by a few powerful people.	1 | 2 | 3 | 4 | 5 | 6 | 7
I believe that honesty is the basis for trust.	1 | 2 | 3 | 4 | 5 | 6 | 7
I believe that giving is more important than receiving.	1 | 2 | 3 | 4 | 5 | 6 | 7
I believe that by working hard a person can achieve anything.	1 | 2 | 3 | 4 | 5 | 6 | 7
I believe that criminals should receive help rather than punishment.	1 | 2 | 3 | 4 | 5 | 6 | 7
I believe that cheating is ok if you get away with it.	1 | 2 | 3 | 4 | 5 | 6 | 7
I believe that medical tests are often inaccurate.	1 | 2 | 3 | 4 | 5 | 6 | 7
I believe strongly that the world would be a much better place if I had my way.	1 | 2 | 3 | 4 | 5 | 6 | 7
I believe only in myself.	1 | 2 | 3 | 4 | 5 | 6 | 7

I believe that one of the most important achievements in life includes acquiring material possessions.	1 | 2 | 3 | 4 | 5 | 6 | 7
I believe that others are drawn to me because I am humble.	1 | 2 | 3 | 4 | 5 | 6 | 7
I believe that there are no "honest" mistakes - there is always an ulterior motive.	1 | 2 | 3 | 4 | 5 | 6 | 7
I believe that we should be tough on crime.	1 | 2 | 3 | 4 | 5 | 6 | 7
I believe that I am important.	1 | 2 | 3 | 4 | 5 | 6 | 7
I believe that I am better than others.	1 | 2 | 3 | 4 | 5 | 6 | 7
I believe that I know more than most supposed "experts."	1 | 2 | 3 | 4 | 5 | 6 | 7
I believe that I can heal others by sending them thoughts of positive energy.	1 | 2 | 3 | 4 | 5 | 6 | 7
I believe that I am always right.	1 | 2 | 3 | 4 | 5 | 6 | 7
I believe that people are either good or bad.	1 | 2 | 3 | 4 | 5 | 6 | 7
I believe that people are basically moral.	1 | 2 | 3 | 4 | 5 | 6 | 7

I feel that people must earn my trust.	1 | 2 | 3 | 4 | 5 | 6 | 7
I believe that people seldom tell you the whole story.	1 | 2 | 3 | 4 | 5 | 6 | 7
I believe that people often are trying to take advantage of me.	1 | 2 | 3 | 4 | 5 | 6 | 7
I believe that, sooner or later, people always let you down.	1 | 2 | 3 | 4 | 5 | 6 | 7
I believe that both feelings and thinking are important in making decisions and solving problems.	1 | 2 | 3 | 4 | 5 | 6 | 7
I believe worry causes me to lose sleep.	1 | 2 | 3 | 4 | 5 | 6 | 7
I believe that the only person you can truly trust is yourself.	1 | 2 | 3 | 4 | 5 | 6 | 7
I believe that events in my life are determined only by me.	1 | 2 | 3 | 4 | 5 | 6 | 7
I believe that things go best when people do things the way I do them or want them done.	1 | 2 | 3 | 4 | 5 | 6 | 7
I believe that the things I own say a lot about how well I'm doing in life.	1 | 2 | 3 | 4 | 5 | 6 | 7
I believe that religion is foolish.	1 | 2 | 3 | 4 | 5 | 6 | 7

I believe that my success depends on ability rather than luck.	1 | 2 | 3 | 4 | 5 | 6 | 7
I believe that life is more of a playground than a battlefield.	1 | 2 | 3 | 4 | 5 | 6 | 7
I believe that important decisions should be based on logical reasoning.	1 | 2 | 3 | 4 | 5 | 6 | 7
I believe that human nature is essentially bad.	1 | 2 | 3 | 4 | 5 | 6 | 7
I believe that everything will work out in the end.	1 | 2 | 3 | 4 | 5 | 6 | 7
I believe that the rules don't apply to me.	1 | 2 | 3 | 4 | 5 | 6 | 7
I believe that the end justifies the means.	1 | 2 | 3 | 4 | 5 | 6 | 7
I believe the world would be better off without me.	1 | 2 | 3 | 4 | 5 | 6 | 7
I believe that the poor deserve our sympathy.	1 | 2 | 3 | 4 | 5 | 6 | 7
I believe that it's dangerous to show your real feelings.	1 | 2 | 3 | 4 | 5 | 6 | 7
I believe that laws should be strictly enforced.	1 | 2 | 3 | 4 | 5 | 6 | 7

I believe that my life is much more of a gift than a problem.	1 | 2 | 3 | 4 | 5 | 6 | 7
I believe that it is more important to be myself than to be popular.	1 | 2 | 3 | 4 | 5 | 6 | 7
I believe that children need firm discipline.	1 | 2 | 3 | 4 | 5 | 6 | 7
I believe that there are universal truths.	1 | 2 | 3 | 4 | 5 | 6 | 7
I believe that some people are born lucky.	1 | 2 | 3 | 4 | 5 | 6 | 7
I believe that there are many sides to most issues.	1 | 2 | 3 | 4 | 5 | 6 | 7
I believe in a logical answer for everything.	1 | 2 | 3 | 4 | 5 | 6 | 7
I believe that each person has a purpose in life.	1 | 2 | 3 | 4 | 5 | 6 | 7
I believe that most questions have one right answer.	1 | 2 | 3 | 4 | 5 | 6 | 7
I believe that there is never an excuse for lying.	1 | 2 | 3 | 4 | 5 | 6 | 7
I believe that most people have ulterior motives when doing good deeds.	1 | 2 | 3 | 4 | 5 | 6 | 7

I believe that it's best not to let other people get to know you too well.	1 | 2 | 3 | 4 | 5 | 6 | 7
I believe that it is best to forgive and forget.	1 | 2 | 3 | 4 | 5 | 6 | 7
I believe that we coddle criminals too much.	1 | 2 | 3 | 4 | 5 | 6 | 7
I believe that most people tell the truth.	1 | 2 | 3 | 4 | 5 | 6 | 7
I believe that most people would betray me if I let them.	1 | 2 | 3 | 4 | 5 | 6 | 7
I believe that most people would lie to get ahead.	1 | 2 | 3 | 4 | 5 | 6 | 7
I believe that most people dislike helping other people.	1 | 2 | 3 | 4 | 5 | 6 | 7
I believe that most people stay friends only as long as it is to their advantage.	1 | 2 | 3 | 4 | 5 | 6 | 7
I believe that most people only care about themselves.	1 | 2 | 3 | 4 | 5 | 6 | 7
I believe that privacy is very important.	1 | 2 | 3 | 4 | 5 | 6 | 7
I blame myself for anything that goes wrong.	1 | 2 | 3 | 4 | 5 | 6 | 7

I waste my time.	1 | 2 | 3 | 4 | 5 | 6 | 7
I express my happiness in a childlike manner.	1 | 2 | 3 | 4 | 5 | 6 | 7
I express my affection physically.	1 | 2 | 3 | 4 | 5 | 6 | 7
I express myself easily.	1 | 2 | 3 | 4 | 5 | 6 | 7
I embarrass others.	1 | 2 | 3 | 4 | 5 | 6 | 7
I express disapproval.	1 | 2 | 3 | 4 | 5 | 6 | 7
I express childlike joy.	1 | 2 | 3 | 4 | 5 | 6 | 7
I do my tasks only just before they need to be done.	1 | 2 | 3 | 4 | 5 | 6 | 7
I do unpleasant tasks immediately.	1 | 2 | 3 | 4 | 5 | 6 | 7
I disclose my intimate thoughts.	1 | 2 | 3 | 4 | 5 | 6 | 7
I find out things quickly.	1 | 2 | 3 | 4 | 5 | 6 | 7

I defend my own beliefs.	1 | 2 | 3 | 4 | 5 | 6 | 7
I come straight to the point.	1 | 2 | 3 | 4 | 5 | 6 | 7
I admit when I am wrong.	1 | 2 | 3 | 4 | 5 | 6 | 7
I express my thanks to those who care about me.	1 | 2 | 3 | 4 | 5 | 6 | 7
I am often aware how the color and lighting of a room affects my mood.	1 | 2 | 3 | 4 | 5 | 6 | 7
I am aware of how my feelings are affecting other people.	1 | 2 | 3 | 4 | 5 | 6 | 7
I am aware of my feelings.	1 | 2 | 3 | 4 | 5 | 6 | 7
I am guided by my intuitions.	1 | 2 | 3 | 4 | 5 | 6 | 7
I forgo things for the sake of others.	1 | 2 | 3 | 4 | 5 | 6 | 7
I forego things that are bad for me in the long run even if they make me feel good in the short run.	1 | 2 | 3 | 4 | 5 | 6 | 7
I am a strange person.	1 | 2 | 3 | 4 | 5 | 6 | 7

I am easily annoyed.	1 | 2 | 3 | 4 | 5 | 6 | 7
I am annoyed by others' mistakes.	1 | 2 | 3 | 4 | 5 | 6 | 7
I am ready for a fight when someone tries to take advantage of me.	1 | 2 | 3 | 4 | 5 | 6 | 7
I am ready to hit someone when I get angry.	1 | 2 | 3 | 4 | 5 | 6 | 7
I am willing to make personal sacrifices in order to help people I care about.	1 | 2 | 3 | 4 | 5 | 6 | 7
I am willing to try again and again when I fail at something.	1 | 2 | 3 | 4 | 5 | 6 | 7
I am willing to take a stand.	1 | 2 | 3 | 4 | 5 | 6 | 7
I am willing to make compromises.	1 | 2 | 3 | 4 | 5 | 6 | 7
I am willing to take risks to establish a relationship.	1 | 2 | 3 | 4 | 5 | 6 | 7
I am willing to cheat in a game.	1 | 2 | 3 | 4 | 5 | 6 | 7
I am willing to bend the truth if it will benefit me.	1 | 2 | 3 | 4 | 5 | 6 | 7

I am known as a controlling person.	1 | 2 | 3 | 4 | 5 | 6 | 7
I describe lots of irrelevant details when telling a story.	1 | 2 | 3 | 4 | 5 | 6 | 7
I find myself in the same kinds of trouble, time after time.	1 | 2 | 3 | 4 | 5 | 6 | 7
I find myself picking up the mood of others.	1 | 2 | 3 | 4 | 5 | 6 | 7
I find political discussions interesting.	1 | 2 | 3 | 4 | 5 | 6 | 7
I find it necessary to please the people who have power.	1 | 2 | 3 | 4 | 5 | 6 | 7
I find that it takes a lot to make me feel frustrated or irritated.	1 | 2 | 3 | 4 | 5 | 6 | 7
I find that it takes a lot to make me feel angry at someone.	1 | 2 | 3 | 4 | 5 | 6 | 7
I act out my frustrations on others.	1 | 2 | 3 | 4 | 5 | 6 | 7
I cherish mementos.	1 | 2 | 3 | 4 | 5 | 6 | 7
I am fascinated by numbers.	1 | 2 | 3 | 4 | 5 | 6 | 7

I attract attention from the opposite sex.	1 | 2 | 3 | 4 | 5 | 6 | 7
I am committed to principles of justice and equality.	1 | 2 | 3 | 4 | 5 | 6 | 7
I decide things on my own.	1 | 2 | 3 | 4 | 5 | 6 | 7
I am looking for a job.	1 | 2 | 3 | 4 | 5 | 6 | 7
I copy others.	1 | 2 | 3 | 4 | 5 | 6 | 7
I consider my behavior to be pretty average.	1 | 2 | 3 | 4 | 5 | 6 | 7
I consider myself to be a wise person.	1 | 2 | 3 | 4 | 5 | 6 | 7
I consider myself an average person.	1 | 2 | 3 | 4 | 5 | 6 | 7
I consider myself a disabled person.	1 | 2 | 3 | 4 | 5 | 6 | 7
I doubt people who claim to be "healers."	1 | 2 | 3 | 4 | 5 | 6 | 7
I doubt reports of so-called "mystical experiences."	1 | 2 | 3 | 4 | 5 | 6 | 7

I doubt the value of religion.	1 | 2 | 3 | 4 | 5 | 6 | 7
I am a neat freak.	1 | 2 | 3 | 4 | 5 | 6 | 7
I am a workaholic, with little time for fun or pleasure.	1 | 2 | 3 | 4 | 5 | 6 | 7
I acknowledge others' accomplishments.	1 | 2 | 3 | 4 | 5 | 6 | 7
I get impatient when others talk to me about their problems.	1 | 2 | 3 | 4 | 5 | 6 | 7
I am full of ideas.	1 | 2 | 3 | 4 | 5 | 6 | 7
I am filled with doubts about things.	1 | 2 | 3 | 4 | 5 | 6 | 7
I borrow money that I won't pay back.	1 | 2 | 3 | 4 | 5 | 6 | 7
I am quick to blame others when I get into trouble.	1 | 2 | 3 | 4 | 5 | 6 | 7
I am quick to think others don't like me.	1 | 2 | 3 | 4 | 5 | 6 | 7
I am quick to judge others.	1 | 2 | 3 | 4 | 5 | 6 | 7

I am a highly disciplined person.	1 | 2 | 3 | 4 | 5 | 6 | 7
I fulfill my duties without complaining.	1 | 2 | 3 | 4 | 5 | 6 | 7
I come up with bold plans.	1 | 2 | 3 | 4 | 5 | 6 | 7
I come up with excuses to avoid meeting new people.	1 | 2 | 3 | 4 | 5 | 6 | 7
I continue until everything is perfect.	1 | 2 | 3 | 4 | 5 | 6 | 7
I am often exploited by others.	1 | 2 | 3 | 4 | 5 | 6 | 7
I assume that most people lie or cheat to get ahead.	1 | 2 | 3 | 4 | 5 | 6 | 7
I try to avoid speaking in public	1 | 2 | 3 | 4 | 5 | 6 | 7
I try to forgive and forget.	1 | 2 | 3 | 4 | 5 | 6 | 7
I could stare at a painting or picture for hours.	1 | 2 | 3 | 4 | 5 | 6 | 7
I am able to calm myself down quite quickly when upset.	1 | 2 | 3 | 4 | 5 | 6 | 7

I am capable of working alone.	1 | 2 | 3 | 4 | 5 | 6 | 7
I am able to work hard to achieve results that I will only get at a time far in the future.	1 | 2 | 3 | 4 | 5 | 6 | 7
I am able to work hard to solve problems even when it takes a long time.	1 | 2 | 3 | 4 | 5 | 6 | 7
I am able to do most things well enough.	1 | 2 | 3 | 4 | 5 | 6 | 7
I am able to do what I should do, even when I feel scared.	1 | 2 | 3 | 4 | 5 | 6 | 7
I can laugh at myself.	1 | 2 | 3 | 4 | 5 | 6 | 7
I am able to control my cravings.	1 | 2 | 3 | 4 | 5 | 6 | 7
I am able to cooperate with others.	1 | 2 | 3 | 4 | 5 | 6 | 7
I finish things despite obstacles in the way.	1 | 2 | 3 | 4 | 5 | 6 | 7
I finish tasks quickly.	1 | 2 | 3 | 4 | 5 | 6 | 7
I agree to anything.	1 | 2 | 3 | 4 | 5 | 6 | 7

I accept challenging tasks.	1 | 2 | 3 | 4 | 5 | 6 | 7
I easily resist temptations.	1 | 2 | 3 | 4 | 5 | 6 | 7
I adapt easily to new situations.	1 | 2 | 3 | 4 | 5 | 6 | 7
I get along well with people I have just met.	1 | 2 | 3 | 4 | 5 | 6 | 7
I criticize others' shortcomings.	1 | 2 | 3 | 4 | 5 | 6 | 7
I prefer to "live in the moment" rather than plan things out.	1 | 2 | 3 | 4 | 5 | 6 | 7
I cheer people up.	1 | 2 | 3 | 4 | 5 | 6 | 7
I encourage others' criticisms.	1 | 2 | 3 | 4 | 5 | 6 | 7
I am good at making people laugh.	1 | 2 | 3 | 4 | 5 | 6 | 7
I comment loudly about others.	1 | 2 | 3 | 4 | 5 | 6 | 7
I confuse fantasies with real memories.	1 | 2 | 3 | 4 | 5 | 6 | 7

I appreciate people who wait on me.	1 | 2 | 3 | 4 | 5 | 6 | 7
I appreciate all forms of art.	1 | 2 | 3 | 4 | 5 | 6 | 7
I appreciate the viewpoints of others.	1 | 2 | 3 | 4 | 5 | 6 | 7
I appreciate good manners.	1 | 2 | 3 | 4 | 5 | 6 | 7
I am afraid of being left alone.	1 | 2 | 3 | 4 | 5 | 6 | 7
I chatter away aimlessly.	1 | 2 | 3 | 4 | 5 | 6 | 7
I will spread false rumors as a way to hurt others.	1 | 2 | 3 | 4 | 5 | 6 | 7
I exert my authority.	1 | 2 | 3 | 4 | 5 | 6 | 7
I doubt the motives of others when I am complimented.	1 | 2 | 3 | 4 | 5 | 6 | 7
I break my promises.	1 | 2 | 3 | 4 | 5 | 6 | 7
I excel in what I do.	1 | 2 | 3 | 4 | 5 | 6 | 7

I expect nothing less than perfection.	1 | 2 | 3 | 4 | 5 | 6 | 7
I expect the worst.	1 | 2 | 3 | 4 | 5 | 6 | 7
I expect things to fail.	1 | 2 | 3 | 4 | 5 | 6 | 7
I am looking forward to things that are coming in the future.	1 | 2 | 3 | 4 | 5 | 6 | 7
I expect others to thank me for generous things that I do for them.	1 | 2 | 3 | 4 | 5 | 6 | 7
I expect people not to like me.	1 | 2 | 3 | 4 | 5 | 6 | 7
I accept people as they are.	1 | 2 | 3 | 4 | 5 | 6 | 7
I accept the consequences of my actions.	1 | 2 | 3 | 4 | 5 | 6 | 7
I accept the consequences of my actions.	1 | 2 | 3 | 4 | 5 | 6 | 7
I accept what others say about me.	1 | 2 | 3 | 4 | 5 | 6 | 7
I make decisions quickly.	1 | 2 | 3 | 4 | 5 | 6 | 7

I make decisions slowly.	1 | 2 | 3 | 4 | 5 | 6 | 7
I decide things for others.	1 | 2 | 3 | 4 | 5 | 6 | 7
I accept apologies easily.	1 | 2 | 3 | 4 | 5 | 6 | 7
I accept others' weaknesses.	1 | 2 | 3 | 4 | 5 | 6 | 7
I accept little from others.	1 | 2 | 3 | 4 | 5 | 6 | 7
I get a thrill out of doing things that might kill me.	1 | 2 | 3 | 4 | 5 | 6 | 7
I admire people who own expensive homes, cars, or clothes.	1 | 2 | 3 | 4 | 5 | 6 | 7
I feel sympathy for those who are worse off than myself.	1 | 2 | 3 | 4 | 5 | 6 | 7
I feel a responsibility to improve the world in which I live.	1 | 2 | 3 | 4 | 5 | 6 | 7
I feel uneasy and concerned whenever I see a distressed look on a child's face.	1 | 2 | 3 | 4 | 5 | 6 | 7
I feel guilty much of the time.	1 | 2 | 3 | 4 | 5 | 6 | 7

I feel guilty as if I had committed a crime, although I did not really commit one.	1 | 2 | 3 | 4 | 5 | 6 | 7
I feel guilty when I say "no."	1 | 2 | 3 | 4 | 5 | 6 | 7
I feel guilty when I believe that I have hurt someone's feelings.	1 | 2 | 3 | 4 | 5 | 6 | 7
I feel guilty when I see a policeman.	1 | 2 | 3 | 4 | 5 | 6 | 7
I am secure in my relationships.	1 | 2 | 3 | 4 | 5 | 6 | 7
I feel comfortable with myself.	1 | 2 | 3 | 4 | 5 | 6 | 7
I feel lucky most of the time.	1 | 2 | 3 | 4 | 5 | 6 | 7
I feel healthy and vibrant most of the time.	1 | 2 | 3 | 4 | 5 | 6 | 7
I feel relieved after inflicting pain on myself.	1 | 2 | 3 | 4 | 5 | 6 | 7
I feel hollow, empty, or bored.	1 | 2 | 3 | 4 | 5 | 6 | 7
I feel weak.	1 | 2 | 3 | 4 | 5 | 6 | 7

I feel smothered when others show deep concern towards me.	1 | 2 | 3 | 4 | 5 | 6 | 7
I feel restless a lot of the time.	1 | 2 | 3 | 4 | 5 | 6 | 7
I feel good when others notice how I have hurt myself.	1 | 2 | 3 | 4 | 5 | 6 | 7
I feel happy when I see other people display their skills and talents.	1 | 2 | 3 | 4 | 5 | 6 | 7
I feel happy when I see a happy animal such as a playful dog or a purring cat.	1 | 2 | 3 | 4 | 5 | 6 | 7
I feel better after some hard work.	1 | 2 | 3 | 4 | 5 | 6 | 7
I feel as if my body, or a part of it, has disappeared.	1 | 2 | 3 | 4 | 5 | 6 | 7
I feel like my imagination can run wild.	1 | 2 | 3 | 4 | 5 | 6 | 7
I feel like nothing seems like fun to me.	1 | 2 | 3 | 4 | 5 | 6 | 7
I feel like a young person.	1 | 2 | 3 | 4 | 5 | 6 | 7
I feel like a loser if I compromise.	1 | 2 | 3 | 4 | 5 | 6 | 7

I feel like a failure when someone else succeeds.	1 | 2 | 3 | 4 | 5 | 6 | 7
I feel like an imposter.	1 | 2 | 3 | 4 | 5 | 6 | 7
I feel uncomfortable when told that I am important.	1 | 2 | 3 | 4 | 5 | 6 | 7
I feel completely overwhelmed when things don't go as planned.	1 | 2 | 3 | 4 | 5 | 6 | 7
I feel at times that I have left my body and am somehow outside my physical self.	1 | 2 | 3 | 4 | 5 | 6 | 7
I feel sometimes that I all-of-a-sudden am in a strange place.	1 | 2 | 3 | 4 | 5 | 6 | 7
I feel sometimes that a part of my body is separate from the rest of me.	1 | 2 | 3 | 4 | 5 | 6 | 7
I feel threatened easily.	1 | 2 | 3 | 4 | 5 | 6 | 7
I feel happy when I see other people doing things like showing compassion, forgiving others, or being kind.	1 | 2 | 3 | 4 | 5 | 6 | 7
I feel older than my age.	1 | 2 | 3 | 4 | 5 | 6 | 7
I feel isolated from other people.	1 | 2 | 3 | 4 | 5 | 6 | 7

I feel attacked by others.	1 | 2 | 3 | 4 | 5 | 6 | 7
I feel spiritually connected to other people.	1 | 2 | 3 | 4 | 5 | 6 | 7
I feel paralyzed for awhile.	1 | 2 | 3 | 4 | 5 | 6 | 7
I feel desperate.	1 | 2 | 3 | 4 | 5 | 6 | 7
I feel controlled by powerful people.	1 | 2 | 3 | 4 | 5 | 6 | 7
I feel offended by forms of discrimination.	1 | 2 | 3 | 4 | 5 | 6 | 7
I feel emotionally damaged.	1 | 2 | 3 | 4 | 5 | 6 | 7
I feel a strong need to hold on to my possessions.	1 | 2 | 3 | 4 | 5 | 6 | 7
I feel compelled to count while I am doing things.	1 | 2 | 3 | 4 | 5 | 6 | 7
I actually get cold when I think of something cold.	1 | 2 | 3 | 4 | 5 | 6 | 7
I feel emotions with extreme intensity.	1 | 2 | 3 | 4 | 5 | 6 | 7

I feel others' emotions.	1 | 2 | 3 | 4 | 5 | 6 | 7
I feel empty in my relationships.	1 | 2 | 3 | 4 | 5 | 6 | 7
I feel badly if my words or actions cause someone else to feel emotional pain.	1 | 2 | 3 | 4 | 5 | 6 | 7
I feel disgusted by anything relating to sex.	1 | 2 | 3 | 4 | 5 | 6 | 7
I feel I have no control over my thoughts.	1 | 2 | 3 | 4 | 5 | 6 | 7
I feel like I have no control over what comes out of my mouth.	1 | 2 | 3 | 4 | 5 | 6 | 7
I feel like I am "falling apart".	1 | 2 | 3 | 4 | 5 | 6 | 7
I feel that I am too tall.	1 | 2 | 3 | 4 | 5 | 6 | 7
I feel that I'm living in a dream, or see my life before me as if it were a movie.	1 | 2 | 3 | 4 | 5 | 6 | 7
I feel that I am too short.	1 | 2 | 3 | 4 | 5 | 6 | 7
I feel that I have to repeat certain numbers.	1 | 2 | 3 | 4 | 5 | 6 | 7

I feel that I am too small.	1 | 2 | 3 | 4 | 5 | 6 | 7
I feel that I am too skinny.	1 | 2 | 3 | 4 | 5 | 6 | 7
I feel that I am too fat.	1 | 2 | 3 | 4 | 5 | 6 | 7
I feel that other people are often to blame for my problems.	1 | 2 | 3 | 4 | 5 | 6 | 7
I feel that others can't figure out what I'm trying to say.	1 | 2 | 3 | 4 | 5 | 6 | 7
I feel that others misunderstand me.	1 | 2 | 3 | 4 | 5 | 6 | 7
I feel that others are beneath me.	1 | 2 | 3 | 4 | 5 | 6 | 7
I feel that people have a hard time understanding me.	1 | 2 | 3 | 4 | 5 | 6 | 7
I feel that people are against me.	1 | 2 | 3 | 4 | 5 | 6 | 7
I feel that people are too dependent on me.	1 | 2 | 3 | 4 | 5 | 6 | 7
I feel that no one tells the truth anymore.	1 | 2 | 3 | 4 | 5 | 6 | 7

I feel that most bad things that happen have a hidden gift in them.	1 | 2 | 3 | 4 | 5 | 6 | 7
I feel that my body is too large.	1 | 2 | 3 | 4 | 5 | 6 | 7
I feel that the slightest problems are the "end of the world."	1 | 2 | 3 | 4 | 5 | 6 | 7
I feel that many things are outside my control.	1 | 2 | 3 | 4 | 5 | 6 | 7
I feel that my interests change quickly.	1 | 2 | 3 | 4 | 5 | 6 | 7
I feel that my body is dissolving or that a part of my body is missing or changing.	1 | 2 | 3 | 4 | 5 | 6 | 7
I feel that the things I own aren't all that important to me.	1 | 2 | 3 | 4 | 5 | 6 | 7
I feel life is boring or bland.	1 | 2 | 3 | 4 | 5 | 6 | 7
I feel that work is not an important part of my life.	1 | 2 | 3 | 4 | 5 | 6 | 7
I feel that breaking the law is okay as long as you don't get caught.	1 | 2 | 3 | 4 | 5 | 6 | 7
I feel that having close friends is not especially important to me.	1 | 2 | 3 | 4 | 5 | 6 | 7

I feel that my life lacks direction.	1 | 2 | 3 | 4 | 5 | 6 | 7
I feel that my life would be better if I owned certain things I don't have	1 | 2 | 3 | 4 | 5 | 6 | 7
I feel it's important to live in a world of beauty.	1 | 2 | 3 | 4 | 5 | 6 | 7
I feel that there are many things that I do not know much about.	1 | 2 | 3 | 4 | 5 | 6 | 7
I feel that I have a lot of inner strength.	1 | 2 | 3 | 4 | 5 | 6 | 7
I feel that there are good and bad numbers.	1 | 2 | 3 | 4 | 5 | 6 | 7
I feel that friendly people are actually trying to manipulate me.	1 | 2 | 3 | 4 | 5 | 6 | 7
I feel that a deadly disease is always around the corner.	1 | 2 | 3 | 4 | 5 | 6 | 7
I feel short-changed in life.	1 | 2 | 3 | 4 | 5 | 6 | 7
I feel that very few merchants take advantage of their customers.	1 | 2 | 3 | 4 | 5 | 6 | 7
I feel that I have done something wrong.	1 | 2 | 3 | 4 | 5 | 6 | 7

I feel that fantasy is more powerful than reality.	1 | 2 | 3 | 4 | 5 | 6 | 7
I feel that too much modesty gets a person in trouble.	1 | 2 | 3 | 4 | 5 | 6 | 7
I feel that the pace of life is too fast.	1 | 2 | 3 | 4 | 5 | 6 | 7
I feel that most people are genuine.	1 | 2 | 3 | 4 | 5 | 6 | 7
I feel a strong sense of oneness with everything around me.	1 | 2 | 3 | 4 | 5 | 6 | 7
I feel a sense of not being real.	1 | 2 | 3 | 4 | 5 | 6 | 7
I feel a special sense of destiny or prophecy.	1 | 2 | 3 | 4 | 5 | 6 | 7
I feel a profound sense of appreciation every day.	1 | 2 | 3 | 4 | 5 | 6 | 7
I feel a sense of worthlessness or hopelessness.	1 | 2 | 3 | 4 | 5 | 6 | 7
I feel like nothing seems interesting to me.	1 | 2 | 3 | 4 | 5 | 6 | 7
I feel I get so engrossed in fantasies that I lose track of reality.	1 | 2 | 3 | 4 | 5 | 6 | 7

I feel that my opinion is worthless unless told otherwise	1 | 2 | 3 | 4 | 5 | 6 | 7
I feel that my worry and anxiety is out of control.	1 | 2 | 3 | 4 | 5 | 6 | 7
I feel that my anxiety overwhelms me.	1 | 2 | 3 | 4 | 5 | 6 | 7
I feel like I wouldn't know what to do if I developed a serious illness.	1 | 2 | 3 | 4 | 5 | 6 | 7
I feel nothing is ever my fault.	1 | 2 | 3 | 4 | 5 | 6 | 7
I am content with my life.	1 | 2 | 3 | 4 | 5 | 6 | 7
I am satisfied with my life.	1 | 2 | 3 | 4 | 5 | 6 | 7
I enjoy being thought of as a normal "mainstream" person.	1 | 2 | 3 | 4 | 5 | 6 | 7
I gossip about others.	1 | 2 | 3 | 4 | 5 | 6 | 7
I cheat on people who have trusted me.	1 | 2 | 3 | 4 | 5 | 6 | 7
I deceive people.	1 | 2 | 3 | 4 | 5 | 6 | 7

I cheat to get ahead.	1 | 2 | 3 | 4 | 5 | 6 | 7
I allow others to walk all over me.	1 | 2 | 3 | 4 | 5 | 6 | 7
I am convinced that I am dying.	1 | 2 | 3 | 4 | 5 | 6 | 7
I am convinced that my way is the best way.	1 | 2 | 3 | 4 | 5 | 6 | 7
I am convinced my doctor is lying to me.	1 | 2 | 3 | 4 | 5 | 6 | 7
I am often bored while working.	1 | 2 | 3 | 4 | 5 | 6 | 7
I am paralyzed by a fear of rejection.	1 | 2 | 3 | 4 | 5 | 6 | 7
I am paralyzed by a fear of being alone.	1 | 2 | 3 | 4 | 5 | 6 | 7
I am resigned to my fate.	1 | 2 | 3 | 4 | 5 | 6 | 7
I change my mood a lot.	1 | 2 | 3 | 4 | 5 | 6 | 7
I change myself to suit others.	1 | 2 | 3 | 4 | 5 | 6 | 7

I avoid being a bother to anyone.	1 | 2 | 3 | 4 | 5 | 6 | 7
I crave romantic touch.	1 | 2 | 3 | 4 | 5 | 6 | 7
I control others by my anger.	1 | 2 | 3 | 4 | 5 | 6 | 7
I discuss my health problems with my family and friends.	1 | 2 | 3 | 4 | 5 | 6 | 7
I conform to others' opinions.	1 | 2 | 3 | 4 | 5 | 6 | 7
I am ashamed of myself.	1 | 2 | 3 | 4 | 5 | 6 | 7
I am able to get over it quickly when someone hurts my feelings.	1 | 2 | 3 | 4 | 5 | 6 | 7
I begin to panic when there is danger.	1 | 2 | 3 | 4 | 5 | 6 | 7
I begin to answer before the other person finishes the question.	1 | 2 | 3 | 4 | 5 | 6 | 7
I avoid contacts with others.	1 | 2 | 3 | 4 | 5 | 6 | 7
I am easily discouraged.	1 | 2 | 3 | 4 | 5 | 6 | 7

I dress to attract sexual attention.	1 | 2 | 3 | 4 | 5 | 6 | 7
I dress to make an impression.	1 | 2 | 3 | 4 | 5 | 6 | 7
I face problems directly.	1 | 2 | 3 | 4 | 5 | 6 | 7
I indulge in my fantasies.	1 | 2 | 3 | 4 | 5 | 6 | 7
I generally focus on the negative side of things.	1 | 2 | 3 | 4 | 5 | 6 | 7
I act or feel in a way that does not fit me.	1 | 2 | 3 | 4 | 5 | 6 | 7
I act impulsively when something is bothering me.	1 | 2 | 3 | 4 | 5 | 6 | 7
I act with hesitation.	1 | 2 | 3 | 4 | 5 | 6 | 7
I act comfortably with others.	1 | 2 | 3 | 4 | 5 | 6 | 7
I act as if I'm constantly on stage.	1 | 2 | 3 | 4 | 5 | 6 | 7
I act as if I'm constantly on stage.	1 | 2 | 3 | 4 | 5 | 6 | 7

I act as if I'm somebody else and completely identify myself with the part.	1 | 2 | 3 | 4 | 5 | 6 | 7
I act as if some laws do not apply to me.	1 | 2 | 3 | 4 | 5 | 6 | 7
I act like people older than me.	1 | 2 | 3 | 4 | 5 | 6 | 7
I act like people younger than me.	1 | 2 | 3 | 4 | 5 | 6 | 7
I act like different people in different situations.	1 | 2 | 3 | 4 | 5 | 6 | 7
I act as I please.	1 | 2 | 3 | 4 | 5 | 6 | 7
I act properly in most situations.	1 | 2 | 3 | 4 | 5 | 6 | 7
I act as a leader.	1 | 2 | 3 | 4 | 5 | 6 | 7
I apologize a lot.	1 | 2 | 3 | 4 | 5 | 6 | 7
I dwell on the past.	1 | 2 | 3 | 4 | 5 | 6 | 7
I disregard the opinions of others.	1 | 2 | 3 | 4 | 5 | 6 | 7

I am interested in people.	1 | 2 | 3 | 4 | 5 | 6 | 7
I am interested in science.	1 | 2 | 3 | 4 | 5 | 6 | 7
I am mainly interested in money.	1 | 2 | 3 | 4 | 5 | 6 | 7
I get annoyed at the slightest provocation.	1 | 2 | 3 | 4 | 5 | 6 | 7
I find it difficult to organize tasks and activities.	1 | 2 | 3 | 4 | 5 | 6 | 7
I find it difficult to touch an object that has been touched by others.	1 | 2 | 3 | 4 | 5 | 6 | 7
I find it difficult to tell whether something really happened, or whether it occurred only in my imagination.	1 | 2 | 3 | 4 | 5 | 6 | 7
I find it hard to know what people are really feeling.	1 | 2 | 3 | 4 | 5 | 6 | 7
I have difficulty understanding abstract ideas.	1 | 2 | 3 | 4 | 5 | 6 | 7
I have difficulty getting rid of nasty thoughts.	1 | 2 | 3 | 4 | 5 | 6 | 7
I have trouble relaxing, even with family or friends.	1 | 2 | 3 | 4 | 5 | 6 | 7

I find it difficult to stay on one course.	1 | 2 | 3 | 4 | 5 | 6 | 7
I find it hard to stay in a bad mood if the people around me are happy.	1 | 2 | 3 | 4 | 5 | 6 | 7
I have difficulty showing affection.	1 | 2 | 3 | 4 | 5 | 6 | 7
I find it difficult showing people that I care about them.	1 | 2 | 3 | 4 | 5 | 6 | 7
I find it difficult showing people that I'm angry with them.	1 | 2 | 3 | 4 | 5 | 6 | 7
I find it difficult to approach others.	1 | 2 | 3 | 4 | 5 | 6 | 7
I find it difficult to telephone someone I do not know.	1 | 2 | 3 | 4 | 5 | 6 | 7
I find it hard to tell others' thoughts by their looks.	1 | 2 | 3 | 4 | 5 | 6 | 7
I find it difficult to sit still for long periods of time.	1 | 2 | 3 | 4 | 5 | 6 | 7
I find it difficult to control my own thoughts.	1 | 2 | 3 | 4 | 5 | 6 | 7
I find it difficult to break my bad habits.	1 | 2 | 3 | 4 | 5 | 6 | 7

I find it hard to describe how I feel about people.	1 | 2 | 3 | 4 | 5 | 6 | 7
I find it difficult to manipulate others.	1 | 2 | 3 | 4 | 5 | 6 | 7
I get upset if others change the way that I have arranged things.	1 | 2 | 3 | 4 | 5 | 6 | 7
I get upset if something is stolen from me, even if it has little monetary value.	1 | 2 | 3 | 4 | 5 | 6 | 7
I am easily excited.	1 | 2 | 3 | 4 | 5 | 6 | 7
I feel excited when I think about the future.	1 | 2 | 3 | 4 | 5 | 6 | 7
I am faithful to old friends.	1 | 2 | 3 | 4 | 5 | 6 | 7
I am true to myself in all circumstances.	1 | 2 | 3 | 4 | 5 | 6 | 7
I am true to my own values.	1 | 2 | 3 | 4 | 5 | 6 | 7
I am embarrassed by praise.	1 | 2 | 3 | 4 | 5 | 6 | 7
I enjoy having control over someone.	1 | 2 | 3 | 4 | 5 | 6 | 7

I enjoy eating in restaurants.	1 | 2 | 3 | 4 | 5 | 6 | 7
I enjoy spending time by myself.	1 | 2 | 3 | 4 | 5 | 6 | 7
I enjoy examining myself and my life.	1 | 2 | 3 | 4 | 5 | 6 | 7
I enjoy discussing movies and books with others.	1 | 2 | 3 | 4 | 5 | 6 | 7
I enjoy imagining what life is like for people in other places or who have lives different from mine.	1 | 2 | 3 | 4 | 5 | 6 | 7
I enjoy feeding animals.	1 | 2 | 3 | 4 | 5 | 6 | 7
I enjoy bringing people together.	1 | 2 | 3 | 4 | 5 | 6 | 7
I enjoy beating the system.	1 | 2 | 3 | 4 | 5 | 6 | 7
I enjoy spending money on things that aren't practical.	1 | 2 | 3 | 4 | 5 | 6 | 7
I enjoy taking my clothes off in front of others.	1 | 2 | 3 | 4 | 5 | 6 | 7
I enjoy being on the go.	1 | 2 | 3 | 4 | 5 | 6 | 7

I enjoy being part of a group.	1 | 2 | 3 | 4 | 5 | 6 | 7
I enjoy being part of a loud crowd.	1 | 2 | 3 | 4 | 5 | 6 | 7
I enjoy being barefoot.	1 | 2 | 3 | 4 | 5 | 6 | 7
I enjoy being reckless.	1 | 2 | 3 | 4 | 5 | 6 | 7
I enjoy feeling "close to the earth."	1 | 2 | 3 | 4 | 5 | 6 | 7
I enjoy using my charm.	1 | 2 | 3 | 4 | 5 | 6 | 7
I enjoy dreaming about a perfect mate.	1 | 2 | 3 | 4 | 5 | 6 | 7
I enjoy taking leisurely strolls.	1 | 2 | 3 | 4 | 5 | 6 | 7
I enjoy going to social gatherings.	1 | 2 | 3 | 4 | 5 | 6 | 7
I enjoy driving fast and passing cars on the highway.	1 | 2 | 3 | 4 | 5 | 6 | 7
I enjoy working with people more than working alone.	1 | 2 | 3 | 4 | 5 | 6 | 7

I enjoy torturing people.	1 | 2 | 3 | 4 | 5 | 6 | 7
I enjoy hurting someone physically.	1 | 2 | 3 | 4 | 5 | 6 | 7
I enjoy flirting with complete strangers.	1 | 2 | 3 | 4 | 5 | 6 | 7
I enjoy injuring myself.	1 | 2 | 3 | 4 | 5 | 6 | 7
I enjoy cartoons.	1 | 2 | 3 | 4 | 5 | 6 | 7
I enjoy reading.	1 | 2 | 3 | 4 | 5 | 6 | 7
I enjoy hearing new ideas.	1 | 2 | 3 | 4 | 5 | 6 | 7
I enjoy manipulating other people's feelings.	1 | 2 | 3 | 4 | 5 | 6 | 7
I enjoy a good ethnic joke among friends.	1 | 2 | 3 | 4 | 5 | 6 | 7
I enjoy crude jokes.	1 | 2 | 3 | 4 | 5 | 6 | 7
I enjoy the warm feeling of being in a group of good friends.	1 | 2 | 3 | 4 | 5 | 6 | 7

I enjoy the beauty of nature.	1 | 2 | 3 | 4 | 5 | 6 | 7
I enjoy my work.	1 | 2 | 3 | 4 | 5 | 6 | 7
I enjoy the thrill that comes with fearful situations.	1 | 2 | 3 | 4 | 5 | 6 | 7
I enjoy contemplation.	1 | 2 | 3 | 4 | 5 | 6 | 7
I enjoy the feel of self-inflicted pain.	1 | 2 | 3 | 4 | 5 | 6 | 7
I enjoy physical exercise.	1 | 2 | 3 | 4 | 5 | 6 | 7
I enjoy elaborate ceremonies.	1 | 2 | 3 | 4 | 5 | 6 | 7
I enjoy science fiction.	1 | 2 | 3 | 4 | 5 | 6 | 7
I enjoy games of strategy.	1 | 2 | 3 | 4 | 5 | 6 | 7
I enjoy intellectual games.	1 | 2 | 3 | 4 | 5 | 6 | 7
I enjoy thought-provoking movies.	1 | 2 | 3 | 4 | 5 | 6 | 7

I enjoy teamwork.	1 | 2 | 3 | 4 | 5 | 6 | 7
I enjoy a good brawl.	1 | 2 | 3 | 4 | 5 | 6 | 7
I enjoy silence.	1 | 2 | 3 | 4 | 5 | 6 | 7
I enjoy reflecting on past events.	1 | 2 | 3 | 4 | 5 | 6 | 7
I am prone to addiction.	1 | 2 | 3 | 4 | 5 | 6 | 7
I am prone to bouts of rage.	1 | 2 | 3 | 4 | 5 | 6 | 7
I am inclined to forgive others.	1 | 2 | 3 | 4 | 5 | 6 | 7
I am careful to avoid making mistakes.	1 | 2 | 3 | 4 | 5 | 6 | 7
I am wary of others.	1 | 2 | 3 | 4 | 5 | 6 | 7
I am determined to finish a task when I start it.	1 | 2 | 3 | 4 | 5 | 6 | 7
I am nice to people I should be angry at.	1 | 2 | 3 | 4 | 5 | 6 | 7

I am considered attractive by others.	1 | 2 | 3 | 4 | 5 | 6 | 7
I am considered to be a wise person.	1 | 2 | 3 | 4 | 5 | 6 | 7
I am considered by others to be weird.	1 | 2 | 3 | 4 | 5 | 6 | 7
I avoid responsibilities.	1 | 2 | 3 | 4 | 5 | 6 | 7
I avoid romantic intimacy at all costs.	1 | 2 | 3 | 4 | 5 | 6 | 7
I avoid mistakes.	1 | 2 | 3 | 4 | 5 | 6 | 7
I dislike having authority over others.	1 | 2 | 3 | 4 | 5 | 6 | 7
I avoid interfering in the lives of others.	1 | 2 | 3 | 4 | 5 | 6 | 7
I avoid throwing things away for fear that I might need them later.	1 | 2 | 3 | 4 | 5 | 6 | 7
I avoid imposing my will on others.	1 | 2 | 3 | 4 | 5 | 6 | 7
I avoid going to unknown places.	1 | 2 | 3 | 4 | 5 | 6 | 7

I avoid dealing with uncomfortable emotions.	1 | 2 | 3 | 4 | 5 | 6 | 7
I avoid doing things behind another person's back.	1 | 2 | 3 | 4 | 5 | 6 | 7
I avoid dangerous situations.	1 | 2 | 3 | 4 | 5 | 6 | 7
I avoid activities that are physically dangerous.	1 | 2 | 3 | 4 | 5 | 6 | 7
I avoid eye contact.	1 | 2 | 3 | 4 | 5 | 6 | 7
I avoid small talk.	1 | 2 | 3 | 4 | 5 | 6 | 7
I avoid philosophical discussions.	1 | 2 | 3 | 4 | 5 | 6 | 7
I am easily offended.	1 | 2 | 3 | 4 | 5 | 6 | 7
I am free of prejudice.	1 | 2 | 3 | 4 | 5 | 6 | 7
I feel excited or happy for no apparent reason.	1 | 2 | 3 | 4 | 5 | 6 | 7
I am thrilled when I learn something new.	1 | 2 | 3 | 4 | 5 | 6 | 7

I am easily deterred.	1 | 2 | 3 | 4 | 5 | 6 | 7
I am easily controlled by others in my life.	1 | 2 | 3 | 4 | 5 | 6 | 7
I am under constant pressure.	1 | 2 | 3 | 4 | 5 | 6 | 7
I am patient with people who annoy me.	1 | 2 | 3 | 4 | 5 | 6 | 7
I don't like getting dirt on my hands.	1 | 2 | 3 | 4 | 5 | 6 | 7
I don't like the idea of change.	1 | 2 | 3 | 4 | 5 | 6 | 7
I count on others too much.	1 | 2 | 3 | 4 | 5 | 6 | 7
I depend on science to explain "miracles."	1 | 2 | 3 | 4 | 5 | 6 | 7
I contradict others.	1 | 2 | 3 | 4 | 5 | 6 | 7
I am just an ordinary person.	1 | 2 | 3 | 4 | 5 | 6 | 7
I am a hard worker.	1 | 2 | 3 | 4 | 5 | 6 | 7

I follow directions.	1 | 2 | 3 | 4 | 5 | 6 | 7
I follow a schedule.	1 | 2 | 3 | 4 | 5 | 6 | 7
I follow my instincts.	1 | 2 | 3 | 4 | 5 | 6 | 7
I do the opposite of what I'm told to do.	1 | 2 | 3 | 4 | 5 | 6 | 7
I do things my own way.	1 | 2 | 3 | 4 | 5 | 6 | 7
I do things for no apparent reason.	1 | 2 | 3 | 4 | 5 | 6 | 7
I do unexpected things.	1 | 2 | 3 | 4 | 5 | 6 | 7
I do things in a logical order.	1 | 2 | 3 | 4 | 5 | 6 | 7
I do things at my own pace.	1 | 2 | 3 | 4 | 5 | 6 | 7
I do things well at first, but then drop them.	1 | 2 | 3 | 4 | 5 | 6 | 7
I do improper things.	1 | 2 | 3 | 4 | 5 | 6 | 7

I do things that are very out of the ordinary.	1 | 2 | 3 | 4 | 5 | 6 | 7
I do things behind other people's backs.	1 | 2 | 3 | 4 | 5 | 6 | 7
I do things out of revenge.	1 | 2 | 3 | 4 | 5 | 6 | 7
I do dangerous things.	1 | 2 | 3 | 4 | 5 | 6 | 7
I do crazy things.	1 | 2 | 3 | 4 | 5 | 6 | 7
I do things out of habit.	1 | 2 | 3 | 4 | 5 | 6 | 7
I do things that others find strange.	1 | 2 | 3 | 4 | 5 | 6 | 7
I do things that I don't like to make others happy.	1 | 2 | 3 | 4 | 5 | 6 | 7
I do things that I later regret.	1 | 2 | 3 | 4 | 5 | 6 | 7
I do things that men traditionally do.	1 | 2 | 3 | 4 | 5 | 6 | 7
I do things that women traditionally do.	1 | 2 | 3 | 4 | 5 | 6 | 7

I do a lot in my spare time.	1 | 2 | 3 | 4 | 5 | 6 | 7
I do a lot of things just to avoid getting sick.	1 | 2 | 3 | 4 | 5 | 6 | 7
I do favors for others only so I can ask for something for myself later.	1 | 2 | 3 | 4 | 5 | 6 | 7
I do more than what's expected of me.	1 | 2 | 3 | 4 | 5 | 6 | 7
I do everything I say I will do.	1 | 2 | 3 | 4 | 5 | 6 | 7
I do my best to avoid arguments.	1 | 2 | 3 | 4 | 5 | 6 | 7
I do as I am told.	1 | 2 | 3 | 4 | 5 | 6 | 7
I do what others do.	1 | 2 | 3 | 4 | 5 | 6 | 7
I do what others want me to do.	1 | 2 | 3 | 4 | 5 | 6 | 7
I do what's expected.	1 | 2 | 3 | 4 | 5 | 6 | 7
I do whatever comes into my mind.	1 | 2 | 3 | 4 | 5 | 6 | 7

I do too little work.	1 | 2 | 3 | 4 | 5 | 6 | 7
I am nervous or tense most of the time.	1 | 2 | 3 | 4 | 5 | 6 | 7
I am sad most of the time.	1 | 2 | 3 | 4 | 5 | 6 | 7
I fear dying from a lingering or painful illness.	1 | 2 | 3 | 4 | 5 | 6 | 7
I blurt out whatever comes into my mind.	1 | 2 | 3 | 4 | 5 | 6 | 7
I act spontaneously without thinking about the consequences.	1 | 2 | 3 | 4 | 5 | 6 | 7
I accomplish a lot of work.	1 | 2 | 3 | 4 | 5 | 6 | 7
I act without consulting others.	1 | 2 | 3 | 4 | 5 | 6 | 7
I act without ulterior motives.	1 | 2 | 3 | 4 | 5 | 6 | 7
I act without planning.	1 | 2 | 3 | 4 | 5 | 6 | 7
I act according to my conscience.	1 | 2 | 3 | 4 | 5 | 6 | 7

I act according to my conscience.	1 | 2 | 3 | 4 | 5 | 6 | 7
I act according to my own feelings.	1 | 2 | 3 | 4 | 5 | 6 | 7
I am guided by my moods.	1 | 2 | 3 | 4 | 5 | 6 | 7
I act at the expense of others.	1 | 2 | 3 | 4 | 5 | 6 | 7
I follow the beaten track.	1 | 2 | 3 | 4 | 5 | 6 | 7
I am a physical coward.	1 | 2 | 3 | 4 | 5 | 6 | 7
I am an eternal pessimist.	1 | 2 | 3 | 4 | 5 | 6 | 7
I am a perfectionist.	1 | 2 | 3 | 4 | 5 | 6 | 7
I easily laugh at myself.	1 | 2 | 3 | 4 | 5 | 6 | 7
I watch too much television.	1 | 2 | 3 | 4 | 5 | 6 | 7
I am a generally obedient person.	1 | 2 | 3 | 4 | 5 | 6 | 7

I consider others' opinions.	1 | 2 | 3 | 4 | 5 | 6 | 7
I am calm even in tense situations.	1 | 2 | 3 | 4 | 5 | 6 | 7
I am relaxed most of the time.	1 | 2 | 3 | 4 | 5 | 6 | 7
I am sensitive to the needs of others.	1 | 2 | 3 | 4 | 5 | 6 | 7
I am very sensitive and easily hurt.	1 | 2 | 3 | 4 | 5 | 6 | 7
I am a money-grubber.	1 | 2 | 3 | 4 | 5 | 6 | 7
I want to prove myself.	1 | 2 | 3 | 4 | 5 | 6 | 7
I am a flamboyant person.	1 | 2 | 3 | 4 | 5 | 6 | 7
I forget appointments.	1 | 2 | 3 | 4 | 5 | 6 | 7
I keep my thoughts to myself.	1 | 2 | 3 | 4 | 5 | 6 | 7
I enjoy my privacy.	1 | 2 | 3 | 4 | 5 | 6 | 7

I am forceful in relationships with friends and family.	1 | 2 | 3 | 4 | 5 | 6 | 7
I dislike incompetence.	1 | 2 | 3 | 4 | 5 | 6 | 7
I detest working.	1 | 2 | 3 | 4 | 5 | 6 | 7
I dread getting up in the morning.	1 | 2 | 3 | 4 | 5 | 6 | 7
I dislike routine.	1 | 2 | 3 | 4 | 5 | 6 | 7
I am different compared to most people.	1 | 2 | 3 | 4 | 5 | 6 | 7
I enjoy offering directions to tourists.	1 | 2 | 3 | 4 | 5 | 6 | 7
I am preoccupied with myself.	1 | 2 | 3 | 4 | 5 | 6 | 7
I am a chronic liar.	1 | 2 | 3 | 4 | 5 | 6 | 7
I am a domineering person.	1 | 2 | 3 | 4 | 5 | 6 | 7
I am dependent on others for things that I should be able to do myself.	1 | 2 | 3 | 4 | 5 | 6 | 7

I am always in the same mood.	1 | 2 | 3 | 4 | 5 | 6 | 7
I am always worried that my partner is going to leave me.	1 | 2 | 3 | 4 | 5 | 6 | 7
I always know why I do things.	1 | 2 | 3 | 4 | 5 | 6 | 7
I always know why I do things.	1 | 2 | 3 | 4 | 5 | 6 | 7
I can always say "enough is enough."	1 | 2 | 3 | 4 | 5 | 6 | 7
I can never find anything.	1 | 2 | 3 | 4 | 5 | 6 | 7
I am always worried about something.	1 | 2 | 3 | 4 | 5 | 6 | 7
I am always ready to start afresh.	1 | 2 | 3 | 4 | 5 | 6 | 7
I complete tasks successfully.	1 | 2 | 3 | 4 | 5 | 6 | 7
I am always busy.	1 | 2 | 3 | 4 | 5 | 6 | 7
I always need to know who my partner is with.	1 | 2 | 3 | 4 | 5 | 6 | 7

I am told that I am too blunt.	1 | 2 | 3 | 4 | 5 | 6 | 7
I can be trusted to keep my promises.	1 | 2 | 3 | 4 | 5 | 6 | 7
I generally doubt the integrity of others.	1 | 2 | 3 | 4 | 5 | 6 | 7
I have deliberately not done my best.	1 | 2 | 3 | 4 | 5 | 6 | 7
I believe that crying helps me feel better.	1 | 2 | 3 | 4 | 5 | 6 | 7
I am afraid to draw attention to myself.	1 | 2 | 3 | 4 | 5 | 6 | 7
I do most of the talking.	1 | 2 | 3 | 4 | 5 | 6 | 7
I found that I could not remember whether I had done something or had just thought about doing that thing.	1 | 2 | 3 | 4 | 5 | 6 | 7
I found that I was able to ignore pain.	1 | 2 | 3 | 4 | 5 | 6 | 7
I found that I became so involved in a fantasy or daydream that it felt like it was really happening to me.	1 | 2 | 3 | 4 | 5 | 6 | 7
I found that when I was watching television or a movie I became so absorbed in the story that I was unaware of other events happening around me.	1 | 2 | 3 | 4 | 5 | 6 | 7

I found that I had no memory for some important event in my life (for example, a wedding or graduation).	1 | 2 | 3 | 4 | 5 | 6 | 7
I have stolen things from time to time.	1 | 2 | 3 | 4 | 5 | 6 | 7
I have stolen things many times.	1 | 2 | 3 | 4 | 5 | 6 | 7
I find life difficult.	1 | 2 | 3 | 4 | 5 | 6 | 7
I had thoughts about death.	1 | 2 | 3 | 4 | 5 | 6 | 7
I have been physically cruel to animals or even other people.	1 | 2 | 3 | 4 | 5 | 6 | 7
I was known for challenging my teachers in school.	1 | 2 | 3 | 4 | 5 | 6 | 7
I have been in trouble for failing to live up to my responsibilities.	1 | 2 | 3 | 4 | 5 | 6 | 7
I was a slow learner in school.	1 | 2 | 3 | 4 | 5 | 6 | 7
I have had the feeling that I was someone else.	1 | 2 | 3 | 4 | 5 | 6 | 7
I have had the feeling that my thoughts were audible.	1 | 2 | 3 | 4 | 5 | 6 | 7

I have had the strange experience in which things seem "more real" than usual.	1 | 2 | 3 | 4 | 5 | 6 | 7
I got in trouble a lot at school.	1 | 2 | 3 | 4 | 5 | 6 | 7
I felt depressed.	1 | 2 | 3 | 4 | 5 | 6 | 7
I felt fearful.	1 | 2 | 3 | 4 | 5 | 6 | 7
I felt close to my parents when I was a child.	1 | 2 | 3 | 4 | 5 | 6 | 7
I felt happy.	1 | 2 | 3 | 4 | 5 | 6 | 7
I treated my parents badly.	1 | 2 | 3 | 4 | 5 | 6 | 7
I have felt the presence of another person when he or she was not really there.	1 | 2 | 3 | 4 | 5 | 6 | 7
I have felt contact with a divine power.	1 | 2 | 3 | 4 | 5 | 6 | 7
I was aware at an early age that I was different from others.	1 | 2 | 3 | 4 | 5 | 6 | 7
I could go months without a thought of sex crossing my mind.	1 | 2 | 3 | 4 | 5 | 6 | 7

I could easily live without having sex.	1 | 2 | 3 | 4 | 5 | 6 | 7
I find fault with everything.	1 | 2 | 3 | 4 | 5 | 6 | 7
I have a dark, depraved, or evil side that I keep to myself.	1 | 2 | 3 | 4 | 5 | 6 | 7
I have a rebellious side that gets me into trouble.	1 | 2 | 3 | 4 | 5 | 6 | 7
I face danger confidently.	1 | 2 | 3 | 4 | 5 | 6 | 7
I have a poor vocabulary.	1 | 2 | 3 | 4 | 5 | 6 | 7
I have a rich vocabulary.	1 | 2 | 3 | 4 | 5 | 6 | 7
I have a strong personality.	1 | 2 | 3 | 4 | 5 | 6 | 7
I have complete confidence in my doctor.	1 | 2 | 3 | 4 | 5 | 6 | 7
I have unusual beliefs about the world.	1 | 2 | 3 | 4 | 5 | 6 | 7
I have secret strategies.	1 | 2 | 3 | 4 | 5 | 6 | 7

I have problems with my eyesight.	1 | 2 | 3 | 4 | 5 | 6 | 7
I have a pleasing physique.	1 | 2 | 3 | 4 | 5 | 6 | 7
I have strong sexual urges.	1 | 2 | 3 | 4 | 5 | 6 | 7
I have strong urges sometimes to hurt myself.	1 | 2 | 3 | 4 | 5 | 6 | 7
I have a very good imagination.	1 | 2 | 3 | 4 | 5 | 6 | 7
I have fixed opinions.	1 | 2 | 3 | 4 | 5 | 6 | 7
I feel that people and things around me are not real.	1 | 2 | 3 | 4 | 5 | 6 | 7
I have a mature view on life.	1 | 2 | 3 | 4 | 5 | 6 | 7
I have a negative view of the world.	1 | 2 | 3 | 4 | 5 | 6 | 7
I have a negative view of the future.	1 | 2 | 3 | 4 | 5 | 6 | 7

Figure Out Your Future

Imagine a person who walks up to a counter at the airport to buy a plane ticket for his next vacation. "Just give me a ticket," he says to the reservation agent. "Anywhere will do."

The agent stares back at him in disbelief. "I'm sorry, sir," she replies. "I'll need some more details. Just minor things–such as the name of your destination city and your arrival and departure dates."

"Oh, I'm not fussy," says the would-be traveler. "I just want to get away. You choose for me."

Now compare this person to another traveler who walks up to the counter and says, "I'd like a ticket to Ixtapa, Mexico, departing on Saturday, March 23, and returning Sunday, April 7. Please give me a window seat, first class, with vegetarian meals."

Ask yourself which traveler is more likely to end up with a vacation that he'll enjoy. The same principle applies in any area of life, and it is especially important for your future. Discovering what you want and having a plan to get there helps you succeed in life, and NLP is a tool to help you get there faster.

The ability to achieve your goals relies heavily on being aware of your true desires. To arrive at a desired location, how fortunate must you be if you simply start walking without knowing where you're going or how you're going to get there? When you have a crystal-clear image of what you want, it's easier to create a solid internal foundation to support it, which in turn makes it easier to take the right actions at the right time, increasing your chances of success. It's critical to document your results. Your central nervous system (CNS) receives a message that this is an important path to take. Your true desires will become clearer as you work through the assignments below.

If you're willing to be completely open and honest with yourself, imagine and write freely a list of 100 things you'd like to accomplish or be in this lifetime - keep in mind that all items must be realistically possible:

1
2
3
4

5
6
7
8
9
10

11
12
13
14
15
16

17
18
19
20
21
22

23
24
25
26
27
28

29
30
31
32
33
34

35
36
37
38
39
40

41
42
43
44
45
46

47
48
49
50
51
52

53

54

55

56

57

58

59
60
61
62
63
64

65
66
67
68
69
70

71
72
73
74
75
76

77
78
79
80
81
82

83
84
85
86
87
88

89
90
91
92
93
94

95
96
97
98
99
100

What does it mean to be happy, for you specifically?

What is your greatest apprehension in life? What are some examples of how you've let fear get in the way of your progress? Because of this fear, how did you avoid embarrassing or uncomfortable situations? In what ways was this fear reflected in your life's philosophy, your worldview, and your faith in yourself?

What items do you need to have with you at all times when you leave the house? What's the reasoning behind this?

Which one of your loved ones do you truly and unwaveringly care for? Who truly and unwaveringly cares for you?

Is there a particular personality trait that you admire most in people you've met? Why? What's so appealing about this trait?

What are some of the things you dislike most about people you know?

Which of your own personality flaws is the most upsetting to you?

What is the flavor that you enjoy the most? Does it have a distinct odor? What kind of emotions and memories does it provoke in you?

What one sentence might well best describe your entire personality? Make a list of possible statements and choose the one that seems to be the most accurate:

Consequently, how would you like to be remembered and talked about in the future?

Is there anything that has been keeping you awake at night lately? What worries and concerns seem to be repetitive throughout the last few years?

Lessons are all around us in life's journey. What is the most important lesson you've learned in your life so far?

With only a few hours to go before you pass away, you've arrived at the end of your journey, sitting on a balcony with your favorite drink and watching the sunset. Smile. You feel as if you've accomplished all that you set out to do in this lifetime, and you take a moment to reflect on all the good that you've done. What exactly are they?

Look at the list of 100 wishful goals you've made earlier, and select 10 specific outcomes, that you feel are the most important to you. Write them here:

1
2
3
4
5
6
7
8
9
10

Make a list of the 10 outcomes in order of importance:

1	
2	
3	
4	
5	
6	
7	
8	
9	
10	

Outcome 1

For outcome #1, write the answer to "If I got that, what would it do for me?". Think about the consequences of achieving each outcome: how would it influence your life? How would you change as a result? How would you feel and think and behave differently than today? How is it going to affect your relationship with other people?

For outcome #1, ask yourself, "Am I more or less motivated to achieve this outcome?" If the answer is "less", change outcome #1 to something more important to you. If it's "more", then describe where in your body your feel this motivation? What sensations do you get, and where exactly, as you think about achieving each specific outcome?

Now take outcome #1, and write it down in this format (replace X with your outcome and Y with what it will do for you): "When I get to X, I would/will Y." Ask yourself: "And when I get Y, what will that do for me?". Write down your answers.

On the surface we all seem to have the same type of outcomes. We each want to earn enough money (or more than enough) to support ourselves and our families. We all want to be happy and have lots of friends. We want to be strong and healthy and attractive. We want to 'figure life out'.

That's the surface structure of our language, what we absorb from our culture, our parents and our wild imagination. Then there's a deep structure, hiding in the background. By exposing this deep structure, we get to experience our true desires and become congruent with our choices.

A student want to succeed in his NLP course, because he wants to change his career and start a coaching business. What will that do for him?

Perhaps he thinks it will give him financial security and more freedom to do as he wishes. And what will THAT do for him?

Maybe financial security is an important value in his life and it will free his mind of worries? And what will THAT do for him?

Being worry free, he believes, would enable him to become more present and aware. And what will THAT do for him?

Being more present and aware, he would experience a stronger connection to other people, especially his children. And what will THAT do for him?

You get the idea... deeper and deeper.

The question "what it will do for me?", gives you the key to unlock the deep hidden meanings of your seemingly earthly outcome. Ask sincerely and repeatedly, for outcome #1, what will the result do for you? And then ask again, what will THAT result do for you?

Take your original outcome #1, and quickly and without thinking, complete the following sentence: "Yes, BUT..."

We'll deal with these objections and obstacles later on, but in the meantime imagine each one of them as a huge rock blocking your path. Give each of them a specific color and a shape:

Take outcome #1 and rewrite it in a positive way. If you outcome is "to lose 10% body fat" or "eliminate my fear of flying", change it to something like, "my body has only 11% fat" and "I enjoy flying":

For outcome #1, answer: how will you know when you've achieved it? What exactly will happen then? What would you see, hear and feel, as this outcome becomes a reality? How would people behave around you? How will you behave around other people?

Think carefully about the context of your outcome #1. If your outcome is to be more passionate with your spouse, it would be only appropriate in certain locations and at certain times, not anywhere and anytime, right? For outcome #1, answer: Exactly when, where and with whom do you wish this outcome to be effective?

Consider the side effects of achieving outcome #1. Is there anything you or others will lose when you achieve this outcome? What are these things? Are you willing to accept the responsibility and consequences? How will you handle these losses?

There's a famous (and true) saying: "If you don't have a plan for your life, you'll end up a part of someone else's plan, and guess what-they don't have your best interests in mind." When your outcome depends on other people's choices, your chances are slim and you have to exert a whole lot of effort to get it. "I want other people to respect or admire me," which is unattainable. It is attainable: "I want to behave, think, and handle my affairs in a respectful, authentic, and serious manner." Other people's reactions or choices are made in their heads, not yours.

Ask yourself: "Is achieving this outcome #1 within my control?"

For outcome #1 ask yourself, what skills and abilities and other resources (money, connections, knowledge, etc.) do you have currently, that make it more likely for you to achieve this outcome? Define the resources you will need to achieve outcome. Who can help you and how exactly? What physical items you absolutely need to make progress? What new skills you might have to learn? What information is needed and where will you get it? How much money is required? Be specific and thorough.

For outcome #1, specify: What do you still need to get or ask for, that you don't currently have, in order to achieve this outcome elegantly and promptly?

For outcome #1, specify: Who can help you get what you need to achieve your outcome? How else can you get anything else you need for the achievement of this outcome?

Build a mental representation of outcome #1. Is it possible for you to visualize the final result in your mind? Is it possible for you to see, hear, and feel what it will be like when you 'have it' in the near future? Write a paragraph or two describing this internal image for outcome #1.

Divide outcome #1 to 10 milestones. What are the most important action steps you must take in order to achieve this outcome within a realistic time frame?

1
2
3
4
5

6
7
8
9
10

Do you truly believe that pursuing outcome #1 is important and meaningful? If yes, why exactly? If not, why did you choose this outcome at all? (here you have a chance to rewrite it).

How exactly would you feel ashamed, guilty or anxious if you did less than your best to achieve outcome #1? Describe the inner conversation you will have with yourself if, a year or two from today, you regret not taking the appropriate action steps.

Do you want to achieve outcome #1 for personal reasons, or to please someone else? Is the pursuit of outcome #1 exciting? enjoyable? satisfying? Describe the feelings and sensations you're expecting from the journey towards fulfilling the outcome, from taking courageous actions and building your inner strength in the process.

Does outcome #1 represent a deeply felt personal dream? How would the disciplined and successful achievement of outcome #1 change the way that you see yourself?

How would achieving outcome #1 affect the lives of the people around you? Family, relatives, friends, colleagues? How would achieving outcome #1 affect the broader community you live in?

Until when exactly would you like to achieve outcome #1? Be specific. You can change the deadline later. How will you monitor your own behavior to ensure you're making progress towards your desired outcome #1?

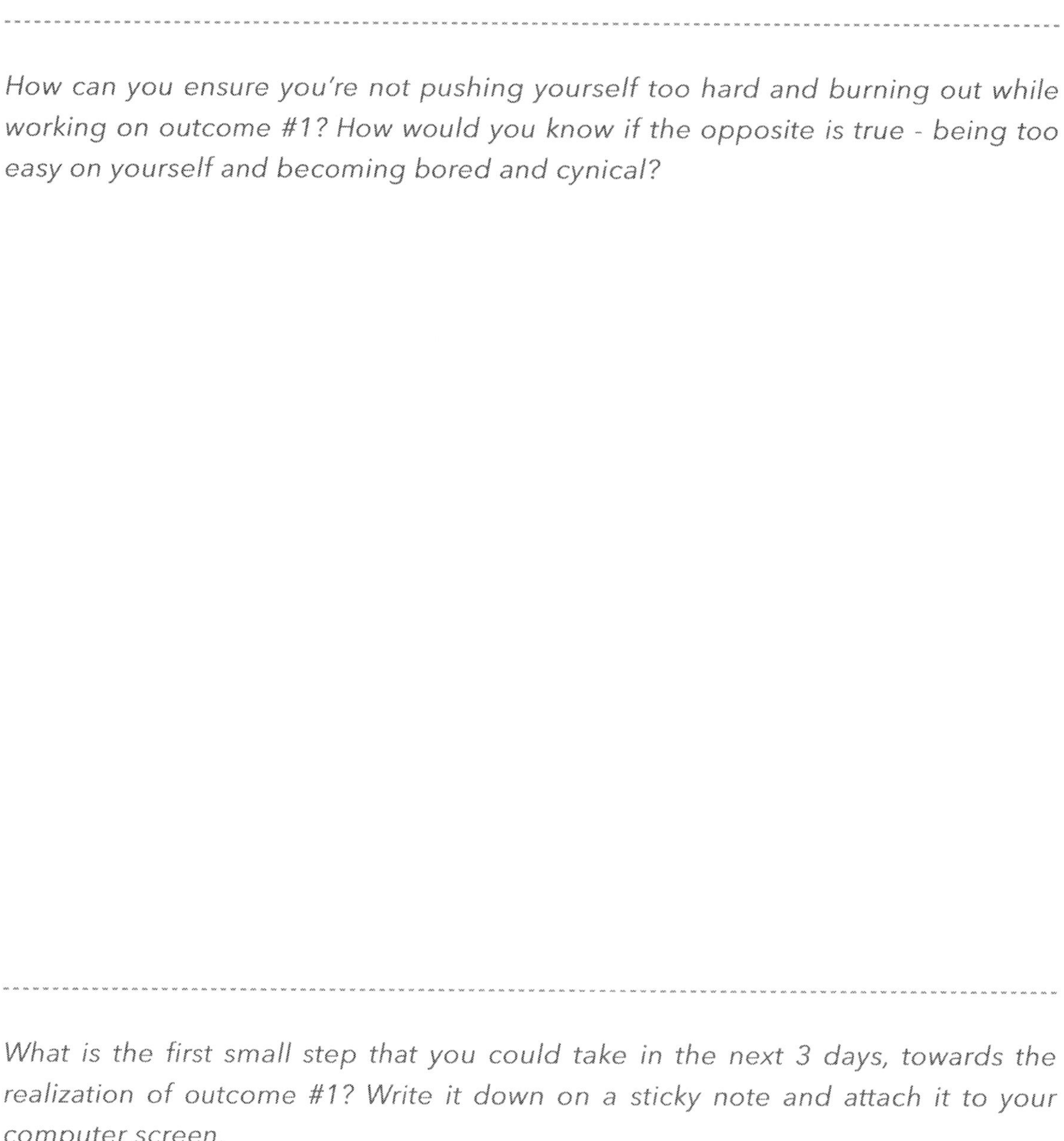

How can you ensure you're not pushing yourself too hard and burning out while working on outcome #1? How would you know if the opposite is true - being too easy on yourself and becoming bored and cynical?

What is the first small step that you could take in the next 3 days, towards the realization of outcome #1? Write it down on a sticky note and attach it to your computer screen.

Outcome 2

For outcome #2, write the answer to "If I got that, what would it do for me?". Think about the consequences of achieving each outcome: how would it influence your life? How would you change as a result? How would you feel and think and behave differently than today? How is it going to affect your relationship with other people?

For outcome #2, ask yourself, "Am I more or less motivated to achieve this outcome?" If the answer is "less", change outcome #2 to something more important to you. If it's "more", then describe where in your body your feel this motivation? What sensations do you get, and where exactly, as you think about achieving each specific outcome?

Now take outcome #2, and write it down in this format (replace X with your outcome and Y with what it will do for you): "When I get to X, I would/will Y." Ask yourself: "And when I get Y, what will that do for me?". Write down your answers.

The question "what it will do for me?", gives you the key to unlock the deep hidden meanings of your seemingly earthly outcome. Ask sincerely and repeatedly, for outcome #2, what will the result do for you? And then ask again, what will THAT result do for you?

Take your original outcome #2, and quickly and without thinking, complete the following sentence: "Yes, BUT..."

We'll deal with these objections and obstacles later on, but in the meantime imagine each one of them as a huge rock blocking your path. Give each of them a specific color and a shape:

Take outcome #2 and rewrite it in a positive way. If you outcome is "to lose 10% body fat" or "eliminate my fear of flying", change it to something like, "my body has only 11% fat" and "I enjoy flying":

For outcome #2, answer: how will you know when you've achieved it? What exactly will happen then? What would you see, hear and feel, as this outcome becomes a reality? How would people behave around you? How will you behave around other people?

Think carefully about the context of your outcome #2. If your outcome is to be more passionate with your spouse, it would be only appropriate in certain locations and at certain times, not anywhere and anytime, right? For outcome #2, answer: Exactly when, where and with whom do you wish this outcome to be effective?

Consider the side effects of achieving outcome #2. Is there anything you or others will lose when you achieve this outcome? What are these things? Are you willing to accept the responsibility and consequences? How will you handle these losses?

Ask yourself: "Is achieving this outcome #2 within my control?"

For outcome #2 ask yourself, what skills and abilities and other resources (money, connections, knowledge, etc.) do you have currently, that make it more likely for you to achieve this outcome? Define the resources you will need to achieve outcome. Who can help you and how exactly? What physical items you absolutely need to make progress? What new skills you might have to learn? What information is needed and where will you get it? How much money is required? Be specific and thorough.

For outcome #2, specify: What do you still need to get or ask for, that you don't currently have, in order to achieve this outcome elegantly and promptly?

For outcome #2, specify: Who can help you get what you need to achieve your outcome? How else can you get anything else you need for the achievement of this outcome?

Build a mental representation of outcome #2. Is it possible for you to visualize the final result in your mind? Is it possible for you to see, hear, and feel what it will be like when you 'have it' in the near future? Write a paragraph or two describing this internal image for outcome #2.

Divide outcome #2 to 10 milestones. What are the most important action steps you must take in order to achieve this outcome within a realistic time frame?

1
2
3
4
5

6
7
8
9
10

Do you truly believe that pursuing outcome #2 is important and meaningful? If yes, why exactly? If not, why did you choose this outcome at all? (here you have a chance to rewrite it).

How exactly would you feel ashamed, guilty or anxious if you did less than your best to achieve outcome #2? Describe the inner conversation you will have with yourself if, a year or two from today, you regret not taking the appropriate action steps.

Do you want to achieve outcome #2 for personal reasons, or to please someone else? Is the pursuit of outcome #2 exciting? enjoyable? satisfying? Describe the feelings and sensations you're expecting from the journey towards fulfilling the outcome, from taking courageous actions and building your inner strength in the process.

Does outcome #2 represent a deeply felt personal dream? How would the disciplined and successful achievement of outcome #2 change the way that you see yourself?

How would achieving outcome #2 affect the lives of the people around you? Family, relatives, friends, colleagues? How would achieving outcome #2 affect the broader community you live in?

Until when exactly would you like to achieve outcome #2? Be specific. You can change the deadline later. How will you monitor your own behavior to ensure you're making progress towards your desired outcome #2?

How can you ensure you're not pushing yourself too hard and burning out while working on outcome #2? How would you know if the opposite is true - being too easy on yourself and becoming bored and cynical?

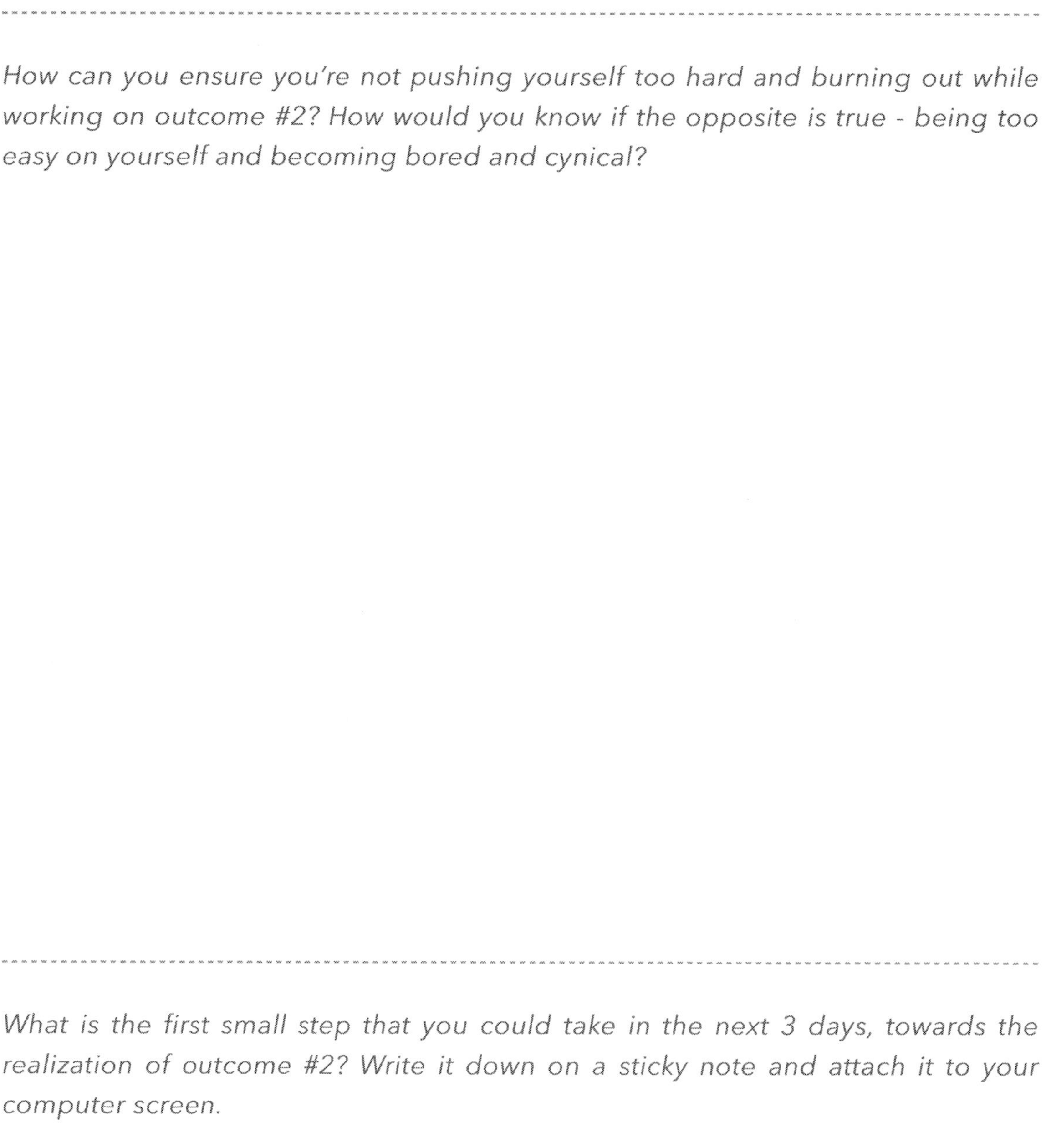

What is the first small step that you could take in the next 3 days, towards the realization of outcome #2? Write it down on a sticky note and attach it to your computer screen.

Outcome 3

For outcome #3, write the answer to "If I got that, what would it do for me?". Think about the consequences of achieving each outcome: how would it influence your life? How would you change as a result? How would you feel and think and behave differently than today? How is it going to affect your relationship with other people?

For outcome #3, ask yourself, "Am I more or less motivated to achieve this outcome?" If the answer is "less", change outcome #3 to something more important to you. If it's "more", then describe where in your body your feel this motivation? What sensations do you get, and where exactly, as you think about achieving each specific outcome?

Now take outcome #3, and write it down in this format (replace X with your outcome and Y with what it will do for you): "When I get to X, I would/will Y." Ask yourself: "And when I get Y, what will that do for me?". Write down your answers.

The question "what it will do for me?", gives you the key to unlock the deep hidden meanings of your seemingly earthly outcome. Ask sincerely and repeatedly, for outcome #3, what will the result do for you? And then ask again, what will THAT result do for you?

Take your original outcome #3, and quickly and without thinking, complete the following sentence: "Yes, BUT..."

We'll deal with these objections and obstacles later on, but in the meantime imagine each one of them as a huge rock blocking your path. Give each of them a specific color and a shape:

Take outcome #3 and rewrite it in a positive way. If you outcome is "to lose 10% body fat" or "eliminate my fear of flying", change it to something like, "my body has only 11% fat" and "I enjoy flying":

For outcome #3, answer: how will you know when you've achieved it? What exactly will happen then? What would you see, hear and feel, as this outcome becomes a reality? How would people behave around you? How will you behave around other people?

Think carefully about the context of your outcome #3. If your outcome is to be more passionate with your spouse, it would be only appropriate in certain locations and at certain times, not anywhere and anytime, right? For outcome #3, answer: Exactly when, where and with whom do you wish this outcome to be effective?

Consider the side effects of achieving outcome #3. Is there anything you or others will lose when you achieve this outcome? What are these things? Are you willing to accept the responsibility and consequences? How will you handle these losses?

Ask yourself: "Is achieving this outcome #3 within my control?"

For outcome #3 ask yourself, what skills and abilities and other resources (money, connections, knowledge, etc.) do you have currently, that make it more likely for you to achieve this outcome? Define the resources you will need to achieve outcome. Who can help you and how exactly? What physical items you absolutely need to make progress? What new skills you might have to learn? What information is needed and where will you get it? How much money is required? Be specific and thorough.

For outcome #3, specify: What do you still need to get or ask for, that you don't currently have, in order to achieve this outcome elegantly and promptly?

For outcome #3, specify: Who can help you get what you need to achieve your outcome? How else can you get anything else you need for the achievement of this outcome?

Build a mental representation of outcome #3. Is it possible for you to visualize the final result in your mind? Is it possible for you to see, hear, and feel what it will be like when you 'have it' in the near future? Write a paragraph or two describing this internal image for outcome #3.

Divide outcome #3 to 10 milestones. What are the most important action steps you must take in order to achieve this outcome within a realistic time frame?

1
2
3
4
5

6
7
8
9
10

Do you truly believe that pursuing outcome #3 is important and meaningful? If yes, why exactly? If not, why did you choose this outcome at all? (here you have a chance to rewrite it).

How exactly would you feel ashamed, guilty or anxious if you did less than your best to achieve outcome #3? Describe the inner conversation you will have with yourself if, a year or two from today, you regret not taking the appropriate action steps.

Do you want to achieve outcome #3 for personal reasons, or to please someone else? Is the pursuit of outcome #3 exciting? enjoyable? satisfying? Describe the feelings and sensations you're expecting from the journey towards fulfilling the outcome, from taking courageous actions and building your inner strength in the process.

Does outcome #3 represent a deeply felt personal dream? How would the disciplined and successful achievement of outcome #3 change the way that you see yourself?

How would achieving outcome #3 affect the lives of the people around you? Family, relatives, friends, colleagues? How would achieving outcome #3 affect the broader community you live in?

Until when exactly would you like to achieve outcome #3? Be specific. You can change the deadline later. How will you monitor your own behavior to ensure you're making progress towards your desired outcome #3?

How can you ensure you're not pushing yourself too hard and burning out while working on outcome #3? How would you know if the opposite is true - being too easy on yourself and becoming bored and cynical?

What is the first small step that you could take in the next 3 days, towards the realization of outcome #3? Write it down on a sticky note and attach it to your computer screen.

Outcome 4

For outcome #4, write the answer to "If I got that, what would it do for me?". Think about the consequences of achieving each outcome: how would it influence your life? How would you change as a result? How would you feel and think and behave differently than today? How is it going to affect your relationship with other people?

For outcome #4, ask yourself, "Am I more or less motivated to achieve this outcome?" If the answer is "less", change outcome #4 to something more important to you. If it's "more", then describe where in your body your feel this motivation? What sensations do you get, and where exactly, as you think about achieving each specific outcome?

Now take outcome #4, and write it down in this format (replace X with your outcome and Y with what it will do for you): "When I get to X, I would/will Y." Ask yourself: "And when I get Y, what will that do for me?". Write down your answers.

The question "what it will do for me?", gives you the key to unlock the deep hidden meanings of your seemingly earthly outcome. Ask sincerely and repeatedly, for outcome #4, what will the result do for you? And then ask again, what will THAT result do for you?

Take your original outcome #4, and quickly and without thinking, complete the following sentence: "Yes, BUT..."

We'll deal with these objections and obstacles later on, but in the meantime imagine each one of them as a huge rock blocking your path. Give each of them a specific color and a shape:

Take outcome #4 and rewrite it in a positive way. If you outcome is "to lose 10% body fat" or "eliminate my fear of flying", change it to something like, "my body has only 11% fat" and "I enjoy flying":

For outcome #4, answer: how will you know when you've achieved it? What exactly will happen then? What would you see, hear and feel, as this outcome becomes a reality? How would people behave around you? How will you behave around other people?

Think carefully about the context of your outcome #4. If your outcome is to be more passionate with your spouse, it would be only appropriate in certain locations and at certain times, not anywhere and anytime, right? For outcome #4, answer: Exactly when, where and with whom do you wish this outcome to be effective?

Consider the side effects of achieving outcome #4. Is there anything you or others will lose when you achieve this outcome? What are these things? Are you willing to accept the responsibility and consequences? How will you handle these losses?

Ask yourself: "Is achieving this outcome #4 within my control?"

For outcome #4 ask yourself, what skills and abilities and other resources (money, connections, knowledge, etc.) do you have currently, that make it more likely for you to achieve this outcome? Define the resources you will need to achieve outcome. Who can help you and how exactly? What physical items you absolutely need to make progress? What new skills you might have to learn? What information is needed and where will you get it? How much money is required? Be specific and thorough.

For outcome #4, specify: What do you still need to get or ask for, that you don't currently have, in order to achieve this outcome elegantly and promptly?

For outcome #4, specify: Who can help you get what you need to achieve your outcome? How else can you get anything else you need for the achievement of this outcome?

Build a mental representation of outcome #4. Is it possible for you to visualize the final result in your mind? Is it possible for you to see, hear, and feel what it will be like when you 'have it' in the near future? Write a paragraph or two describing this internal image for outcome #4.

Divide outcome #4 to 10 milestones. What are the most important action steps you must take in order to achieve this outcome within a realistic time frame?

1
2
3
4
5

6
7
8
9
10

Do you truly believe that pursuing outcome #4 is important and meaningful? If yes, why exactly? If not, why did you choose this outcome at all? (here you have a chance to rewrite it).

How exactly would you feel ashamed, guilty or anxious if you did less than your best to achieve outcome #4? Describe the inner conversation you will have with yourself if, a year or two from today, you regret not taking the appropriate action steps.

Do you want to achieve outcome #4 for personal reasons, or to please someone else? Is the pursuit of outcome #4 exciting? enjoyable? satisfying? Describe the feelings and sensations you're expecting from the journey towards fulfilling the outcome, from taking courageous actions and building your inner strength in the process.

Does outcome #4 represent a deeply felt personal dream? How would the disciplined and successful achievement of outcome #4 change the way that you see yourself?

How would achieving outcome #4 affect the lives of the people around you? Family, relatives, friends, colleagues? How would achieving outcome #4 affect the broader community you live in?

Until when exactly would you like to achieve outcome #4? Be specific. You can change the deadline later. How will you monitor your own behavior to ensure you're making progress towards your desired outcome #4?

How can you ensure you're not pushing yourself too hard and burning out while working on outcome #4? How would you know if the opposite is true - being too easy on yourself and becoming bored and cynical?

What is the first small step that you could take in the next 3 days, towards the realization of outcome #4? Write it down on a sticky note and attach it to your computer screen.

Outcome 5

For outcome #5, write the answer to "If I got that, what would it do for me?". Think about the consequences of achieving each outcome: how would it influence your life? How would you change as a result? How would you feel and think and behave differently than today? How is it going to affect your relationship with other people?

For outcome #5, ask yourself, "Am I more or less motivated to achieve this outcome?" If the answer is "less", change outcome #5 to something more important to you. If it's "more", then describe where in your body your feel this motivation? What sensations do you get, and where exactly, as you think about achieving each specific outcome?

Now take outcome #5, and write it down in this format (replace X with your outcome and Y with what it will do for you): "When I get to X, I would/will Y." Ask yourself: "And when I get Y, what will that do for me?". Write down your answers.

The question "what it will do for me?", gives you the key to unlock the deep hidden meanings of your seemingly earthly outcome. Ask sincerely and repeatedly, for outcome #5, what will the result do for you? And then ask again, what will THAT result do for you?

Take your original outcome #5, and quickly and without thinking, complete the following sentence: "Yes, BUT..."

We'll deal with these objections and obstacles later on, but in the meantime imagine each one of them as a huge rock blocking your path. Give each of them a specific color and a shape:

Take outcome #5 and rewrite it in a positive way. If you outcome is "to lose 10% body fat" or "eliminate my fear of flying", change it to something like, "my body has only 11% fat" and "I enjoy flying":

For outcome #5, answer: how will you know when you've achieved it? What exactly will happen then? What would you see, hear and feel, as this outcome becomes a reality? How would people behave around you? How will you behave around other people?

Think carefully about the context of your outcome #5. If your outcome is to be more passionate with your spouse, it would be only appropriate in certain locations and at certain times, not anywhere and anytime, right? For outcome #5, answer: Exactly when, where and with whom do you wish this outcome to be effective?

Consider the side effects of achieving outcome #5. Is there anything you or others will lose when you achieve this outcome? What are these things? Are you willing to accept the responsibility and consequences? How will you handle these losses?

Ask yourself: "Is achieving this outcome #5 within my control?"

For outcome #5 ask yourself, what skills and abilities and other resources (money, connections, knowledge, etc.) do you have currently, that make it more likely for you to achieve this outcome? Define the resources you will need to achieve outcome. Who can help you and how exactly? What physical items you absolutely need to make progress? What new skills you might have to learn? What information is needed and where will you get it? How much money is required? Be specific and thorough.

For outcome #5, specify: What do you still need to get or ask for, that you don't currently have, in order to achieve this outcome elegantly and promptly?

For outcome #5, specify: Who can help you get what you need to achieve your outcome? How else can you get anything else you need for the achievement of this outcome?

Build a mental representation of outcome #5. Is it possible for you to visualize the final result in your mind? Is it possible for you to see, hear, and feel what it will be like when you 'have it' in the near future? Write a paragraph or two describing this internal image for outcome #5.

Divide outcome #5 to 10 milestones. What are the most important action steps you must take in order to achieve this outcome within a realistic time frame?

1
2
3
4
5

6
7
8
9
10

Do you truly believe that pursuing outcome #5 is important and meaningful? If yes, why exactly? If not, why did you choose this outcome at all? (here you have a chance to rewrite it).

How exactly would you feel ashamed, guilty or anxious if you did less than your best to achieve outcome #5? Describe the inner conversation you will have with yourself if, a year or two from today, you regret not taking the appropriate action steps.

Do you want to achieve outcome #5 for personal reasons, or to please someone else? Is the pursuit of outcome #5 exciting? enjoyable? satisfying? Describe the feelings and sensations you're expecting from the journey towards fulfilling the outcome, from taking courageous actions and building your inner strength in the process.

Does outcome #5 represent a deeply felt personal dream? How would the disciplined and successful achievement of outcome #5 change the way that you see yourself?

How would achieving outcome #5 affect the lives of the people around you? Family, relatives, friends, colleagues? How would achieving outcome #5 affect the broader community you live in?

Until when exactly would you like to achieve outcome #5? Be specific. You can change the deadline later. How will you monitor your own behavior to ensure you're making progress towards your desired outcome #5?

How can you ensure you're not pushing yourself too hard and burning out while working on outcome #5? How would you know if the opposite is true - being too easy on yourself and becoming bored and cynical?

What is the first small step that you could take in the next 3 days, towards the realization of outcome #5? Write it down on a sticky note and attach it to your computer screen.

Outcome 6

For outcome #6, write the answer to "If I got that, what would it do for me?". Think about the consequences of achieving each outcome: how would it influence your life? How would you change as a result? How would you feel and think and behave differently than today? How is it going to affect your relationship with other people?

For outcome #6, ask yourself, "Am I more or less motivated to achieve this outcome?" If the answer is "less", change outcome #6 to something more important to you. If it's "more", then describe where in your body your feel this motivation? What sensations do you get, and where exactly, as you think about achieving each specific outcome?

Now take outcome #6, and write it down in this format (replace X with your outcome and Y with what it will do for you): "When I get to X, I would/will Y." Ask yourself: "And when I get Y, what will that do for me?". Write down your answers.

The question "what it will do for me?", gives you the key to unlock the deep hidden meanings of your seemingly earthly outcome. Ask sincerely and repeatedly, for outcome #6, what will the result do for you? And then ask again, what will THAT result do for you?

Take your original outcome #6, and quickly and without thinking, complete the following sentence: "Yes, BUT..."

We'll deal with these objections and obstacles later on, but in the meantime imagine each one of them as a huge rock blocking your path. Give each of them a specific color and a shape:

Take outcome #6 and rewrite it in a positive way. If you outcome is "to lose 10% body fat" or "eliminate my fear of flying", change it to something like, "my body has only 11% fat" and "I enjoy flying":

For outcome #6, answer: how will you know when you've achieved it? What exactly will happen then? What would you see, hear and feel, as this outcome becomes a reality? How would people behave around you? How will you behave around other people?

Think carefully about the context of your outcome #6. If your outcome is to be more passionate with your spouse, it would be only appropriate in certain locations and at certain times, not anywhere and anytime, right? For outcome #6, answer: Exactly when, where and with whom do you wish this outcome to be effective?

Consider the side effects of achieving outcome #6. Is there anything you or others will lose when you achieve this outcome? What are these things? Are you willing to accept the responsibility and consequences? How will you handle these losses?

Ask yourself: "Is achieving this outcome #6 within my control?"

For outcome #6 ask yourself, what skills and abilities and other resources (money, connections, knowledge, etc.) do you have currently, that make it more likely for you to achieve this outcome? Define the resources you will need to achieve outcome. Who can help you and how exactly? What physical items you absolutely need to make progress? What new skills you might have to learn? What information is needed and where will you get it? How much money is required? Be specific and thorough.

For outcome #6, specify: What do you still need to get or ask for, that you don't currently have, in order to achieve this outcome elegantly and promptly?

For outcome #6, specify: Who can help you get what you need to achieve your outcome? How else can you get anything else you need for the achievement of this outcome?

Build a mental representation of outcome #6. Is it possible for you to visualize the final result in your mind? Is it possible for you to see, hear, and feel what it will be like when you 'have it' in the near future? Write a paragraph or two describing this internal image for outcome #6.

Divide outcome #6 to 10 milestones. What are the most important action steps you must take in order to achieve this outcome within a realistic time frame?

1
2
3
4
5

6
7
8
9
10

Do you truly believe that pursuing outcome #6 is important and meaningful? If yes, why exactly? If not, why did you choose this outcome at all? (here you have a chance to rewrite it).

How exactly would you feel ashamed, guilty or anxious if you did less than your best to achieve outcome #6? Describe the inner conversation you will have with yourself if, a year or two from today, you regret not taking the appropriate action steps.

Do you want to achieve outcome #6 for personal reasons, or to please someone else? Is the pursuit of outcome #6 exciting? enjoyable? satisfying? Describe the feelings and sensations you're expecting from the journey towards fulfilling the outcome, from taking courageous actions and building your inner strength in the process.

Does outcome #6 represent a deeply felt personal dream? How would the disciplined and successful achievement of outcome #6 change the way that you see yourself?

How would achieving outcome #6 affect the lives of the people around you? Family, relatives, friends, colleagues? How would achieving outcome #6 affect the broader community you live in?

Until when exactly would you like to achieve outcome #6? Be specific. You can change the deadline later. How will you monitor your own behavior to ensure you're making progress towards your desired outcome #6?

How can you ensure you're not pushing yourself too hard and burning out while working on outcome #6? How would you know if the opposite is true - being too easy on yourself and becoming bored and cynical?

What is the first small step that you could take in the next 3 days, towards the realization of outcome #6? Write it down on a sticky note and attach it to your computer screen.

Outcome 7

For outcome #7, write the answer to "If I got that, what would it do for me?". Think about the consequences of achieving each outcome: how would it influence your life? How would you change as a result? How would you feel and think and behave differently than today? How is it going to affect your relationship with other people?

For outcome #7, ask yourself, "Am I more or less motivated to achieve this outcome?" If the answer is "less", change outcome #7 to something more important to you. If it's "more", then describe where in your body your feel this motivation? What sensations do you get, and where exactly, as you think about achieving each specific outcome?

Now take outcome #7, and write it down in this format (replace X with your outcome and Y with what it will do for you): "When I get to X, I would/will Y." Ask yourself: "And when I get Y, what will that do for me?". Write down your answers.

The question "what it will do for me?", gives you the key to unlock the deep hidden meanings of your seemingly earthly outcome. Ask sincerely and repeatedly, for outcome #7, what will the result do for you? And then ask again, what will THAT result do for you?

Take your original outcome #7, and quickly and without thinking, complete the following sentence: "Yes, BUT..."

We'll deal with these objections and obstacles later on, but in the meantime imagine each one of them as a huge rock blocking your path. Give each of them a specific color and a shape:

Take outcome #7 and rewrite it in a positive way. If you outcome is "to lose 10% body fat" or "eliminate my fear of flying", change it to something like, "my body has only 11% fat" and "I enjoy flying":

For outcome #7, answer: how will you know when you've achieved it? What exactly will happen then? What would you see, hear and feel, as this outcome becomes a reality? How would people behave around you? How will you behave around other people?

Think carefully about the context of your outcome #7. If your outcome is to be more passionate with your spouse, it would be only appropriate in certain locations and at certain times, not anywhere and anytime, right? For outcome #7, answer: Exactly when, where and with whom do you wish this outcome to be effective?

Consider the side effects of achieving outcome #7. Is there anything you or others will lose when you achieve this outcome? What are these things? Are you willing to accept the responsibility and consequences? How will you handle these losses?

Ask yourself: "Is achieving this outcome #7 within my control?"

For outcome #7 ask yourself, what skills and abilities and other resources (money, connections, knowledge, etc.) do you have currently, that make it more likely for you to achieve this outcome? Define the resources you will need to achieve outcome. Who can help you and how exactly? What physical items you absolutely need to make progress? What new skills you might have to learn? What information is needed and where will you get it? How much money is required? Be specific and thorough.

For outcome #7, specify: What do you still need to get or ask for, that you don't currently have, in order to achieve this outcome elegantly and promptly?

For outcome #7, specify: Who can help you get what you need to achieve your outcome? How else can you get anything else you need for the achievement of this outcome?

Build a mental representation of outcome #7. Is it possible for you to visualize the final result in your mind? Is it possible for you to see, hear, and feel what it will be like when you 'have it' in the near future? Write a paragraph or two describing this internal image for outcome #7.

Divide outcome #7 to 10 milestones. What are the most important action steps you must take in order to achieve this outcome within a realistic time frame?

1
2
3
4
5

6
7
8
9
10

Do you truly believe that pursuing outcome #7 is important and meaningful? If yes, why exactly? If not, why did you choose this outcome at all? (here you have a chance to rewrite it).

How exactly would you feel ashamed, guilty or anxious if you did less than your best to achieve outcome #7? Describe the inner conversation you will have with yourself if, a year or two from today, you regret not taking the appropriate action steps.

Do you want to achieve outcome #7 for personal reasons, or to please someone else? Is the pursuit of outcome #7 exciting? enjoyable? satisfying? Describe the feelings and sensations you're expecting from the journey towards fulfilling the outcome, from taking courageous actions and building your inner strength in the process.

Does outcome #7 represent a deeply felt personal dream? How would the disciplined and successful achievement of outcome #7 change the way that you see yourself?

How would achieving outcome #7 affect the lives of the people around you? Family, relatives, friends, colleagues? How would achieving outcome #7 affect the broader community you live in?

Until when exactly would you like to achieve outcome #7? Be specific. You can change the deadline later. How will you monitor your own behavior to ensure you're making progress towards your desired outcome #7?

How can you ensure you're not pushing yourself too hard and burning out while working on outcome #7? How would you know if the opposite is true - being too easy on yourself and becoming bored and cynical?

What is the first small step that you could take in the next 3 days, towards the realization of outcome #7? Write it down on a sticky note and attach it to your computer screen.

Outcome 8

For outcome #8, write the answer to "If I got that, what would it do for me?". Think about the consequences of achieving each outcome: how would it influence your life? How would you change as a result? How would you feel and think and behave differently than today? How is it going to affect your relationship with other people?

For outcome #8, ask yourself, "Am I more or less motivated to achieve this outcome?" If the answer is "less", change outcome #8 to something more important to you. If it's "more", then describe where in your body your feel this motivation? What sensations do you get, and where exactly, as you think about achieving each specific outcome?

Now take outcome #8, and write it down in this format (replace X with your outcome and Y with what it will do for you): "When I get to X, I would/will Y." Ask yourself: "And when I get Y, what will that do for me?". Write down your answers.

The question "what it will do for me?", gives you the key to unlock the deep hidden meanings of your seemingly earthly outcome. Ask sincerely and repeatedly, for outcome #8, what will the result do for you? And then ask again, what will THAT result do for you?

Take your original outcome #8, and quickly and without thinking, complete the following sentence: "Yes, BUT..."

We'll deal with these objections and obstacles later on, but in the meantime imagine each one of them as a huge rock blocking your path. Give each of them a specific color and a shape:

Take outcome #8 and rewrite it in a positive way. If you outcome is "to lose 10% body fat" or "eliminate my fear of flying", change it to something like, "my body has only 11% fat" and "I enjoy flying":

For outcome #8, answer: how will you know when you've achieved it? What exactly will happen then? What would you see, hear and feel, as this outcome becomes a reality? How would people behave around you? How will you behave around other people?

Think carefully about the context of your outcome #8. If your outcome is to be more passionate with your spouse, it would be only appropriate in certain locations and at certain times, not anywhere and anytime, right? For outcome #8, answer: Exactly when, where and with whom do you wish this outcome to be effective?

Consider the side effects of achieving outcome #8. Is there anything you or others will lose when you achieve this outcome? What are these things? Are you willing to accept the responsibility and consequences? How will you handle these losses?

Ask yourself: "Is achieving this outcome #8 within my control?"

For outcome #8 ask yourself, what skills and abilities and other resources (money, connections, knowledge, etc.) do you have currently, that make it more likely for you to achieve this outcome? Define the resources you will need to achieve outcome. Who can help you and how exactly? What physical items you absolutely need to make progress? What new skills you might have to learn? What information is needed and where will you get it? How much money is required? Be specific and thorough.

For outcome #8, specify: What do you still need to get or ask for, that you don't currently have, in order to achieve this outcome elegantly and promptly?

For outcome #8, specify: Who can help you get what you need to achieve your outcome? How else can you get anything else you need for the achievement of this outcome?

Build a mental representation of outcome #8. Is it possible for you to visualize the final result in your mind? Is it possible for you to see, hear, and feel what it will be like when you 'have it' in the near future? Write a paragraph or two describing this internal image for outcome #8.

Divide outcome #8 to 10 milestones. What are the most important action steps you must take in order to achieve this outcome within a realistic time frame?

1
2
3
4
5

6
7
8
9
10

Do you truly believe that pursuing outcome #8 is important and meaningful? If yes, why exactly? If not, why did you choose this outcome at all? (here you have a chance to rewrite it).

How exactly would you feel ashamed, guilty or anxious if you did less than your best to achieve outcome #8? Describe the inner conversation you will have with yourself if, a year or two from today, you regret not taking the appropriate action steps.

Do you want to achieve outcome #8 for personal reasons, or to please someone else? Is the pursuit of outcome #8 exciting? enjoyable? satisfying? Describe the feelings and sensations you're expecting from the journey towards fulfilling the outcome, from taking courageous actions and building your inner strength in the process.

Does outcome #8 represent a deeply felt personal dream? How would the disciplined and successful achievement of outcome #8 change the way that you see yourself?

How would achieving outcome #8 affect the lives of the people around you? Family, relatives, friends, colleagues? How would achieving outcome #8 affect the broader community you live in?

Until when exactly would you like to achieve outcome #8? Be specific. You can change the deadline later. How will you monitor your own behavior to ensure you're making progress towards your desired outcome #8?

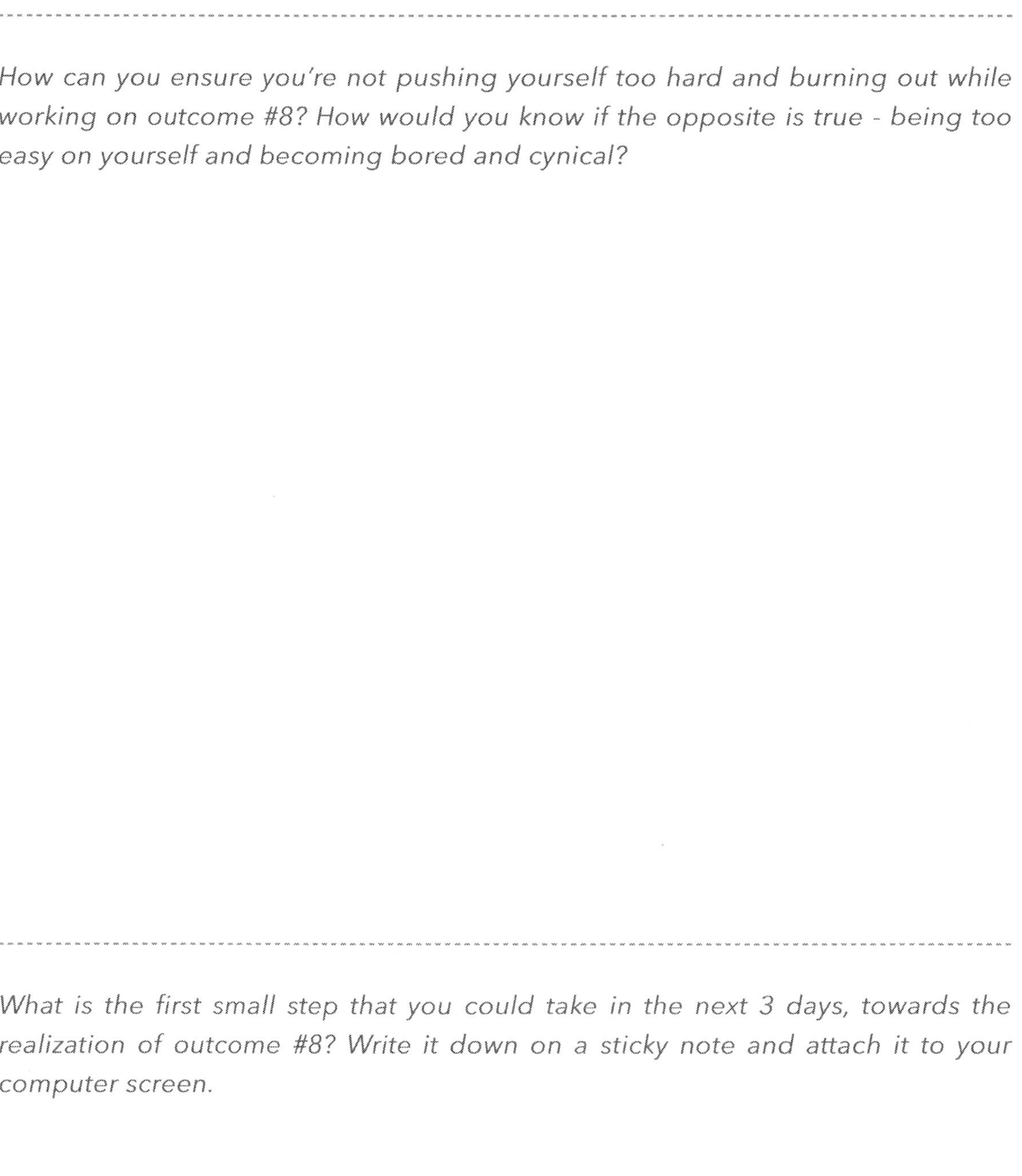

How can you ensure you're not pushing yourself too hard and burning out while working on outcome #8? How would you know if the opposite is true - being too easy on yourself and becoming bored and cynical?

What is the first small step that you could take in the next 3 days, towards the realization of outcome #8? Write it down on a sticky note and attach it to your computer screen.

Outcome 9

For outcome #9, write the answer to "If I got that, what would it do for me?". Think about the consequences of achieving each outcome: how would it influence your life? How would you change as a result? How would you feel and think and behave differently than today? How is it going to affect your relationship with other people?

For outcome #9, ask yourself, "Am I more or less motivated to achieve this outcome?" If the answer is "less", change outcome #9 to something more important to you. If it's "more", then describe where in your body your feel this motivation? What sensations do you get, and where exactly, as you think about achieving each specific outcome?

Now take outcome #9, and write it down in this format (replace X with your outcome and Y with what it will do for you): "When I get to X, I would/will Y." Ask yourself: "And when I get Y, what will that do for me?". Write down your answers.

The question "what it will do for me?", gives you the key to unlock the deep hidden meanings of your seemingly earthly outcome. Ask sincerely and repeatedly, for outcome #9, what will the result do for you? And then ask again, what will THAT result do for you?

Take your original outcome #9, and quickly and without thinking, complete the following sentence: "Yes, BUT..."

We'll deal with these objections and obstacles later on, but in the meantime imagine each one of them as a huge rock blocking your path. Give each of them a specific color and a shape:

Take outcome #9 and rewrite it in a positive way. If you outcome is "to lose 10% body fat" or "eliminate my fear of flying", change it to something like, "my body has only 11% fat" and "I enjoy flying":

For outcome #9, answer: how will you know when you've achieved it? What exactly will happen then? What would you see, hear and feel, as this outcome becomes a reality? How would people behave around you? How will you behave around other people?

Think carefully about the context of your outcome #9. If your outcome is to be more passionate with your spouse, it would be only appropriate in certain locations and at certain times, not anywhere and anytime, right? For outcome #9, answer: Exactly when, where and with whom do you wish this outcome to be effective?

Consider the side effects of achieving outcome #9. Is there anything you or others will lose when you achieve this outcome? What are these things? Are you willing to accept the responsibility and consequences? How will you handle these losses?

Ask yourself: "Is achieving this outcome #9 within my control?"

For outcome #9 ask yourself, what skills and abilities and other resources (money, connections, knowledge, etc.) do you have currently, that make it more likely for you to achieve this outcome? Define the resources you will need to achieve outcome. Who can help you and how exactly? What physical items you absolutely need to make progress? What new skills you might have to learn? What information is needed and where will you get it? How much money is required? Be specific and thorough.

For outcome #9, specify: What do you still need to get or ask for, that you don't currently have, in order to achieve this outcome elegantly and promptly?

For outcome #9, specify: Who can help you get what you need to achieve your outcome? How else can you get anything else you need for the achievement of this outcome?

Build a mental representation of outcome #9. Is it possible for you to visualize the final result in your mind? Is it possible for you to see, hear, and feel what it will be like when you 'have it' in the near future? Write a paragraph or two describing this internal image for outcome #9.

Divide outcome #9 to 10 milestones. What are the most important action steps you must take in order to achieve this outcome within a realistic time frame?

1
2
3
4
5

6
7
8
9
10

Do you truly believe that pursuing outcome #9 is important and meaningful? If yes, why exactly? If not, why did you choose this outcome at all? (here you have a chance to rewrite it).

How exactly would you feel ashamed, guilty or anxious if you did less than your best to achieve outcome #9? Describe the inner conversation you will have with yourself if, a year or two from today, you regret not taking the appropriate action steps.

Do you want to achieve outcome #9 for personal reasons, or to please someone else? Is the pursuit of outcome #9 exciting? enjoyable? satisfying? Describe the feelings and sensations you're expecting from the journey towards fulfilling the outcome, from taking courageous actions and building your inner strength in the process.

Does outcome #9 represent a deeply felt personal dream? How would the disciplined and successful achievement of outcome #9 change the way that you see yourself?

How would achieving outcome #9 affect the lives of the people around you? Family, relatives, friends, colleagues? How would achieving outcome #9 affect the broader community you live in?

Until when exactly would you like to achieve outcome #9? Be specific. You can change the deadline later. How will you monitor your own behavior to ensure you're making progress towards your desired outcome #9?

How can you ensure you're not pushing yourself too hard and burning out while working on outcome #9? How would you know if the opposite is true - being too easy on yourself and becoming bored and cynical?

What is the first small step that you could take in the next 3 days, towards the realization of outcome #9? Write it down on a sticky note and attach it to your computer screen.

Outcome 10

For outcome #10, write the answer to "If I got that, what would it do for me?". Think about the consequences of achieving each outcome: how would it influence your life? How would you change as a result? How would you feel and think and behave differently than today? How is it going to affect your relationship with other people?

For outcome #10, ask yourself, "Am I more or less motivated to achieve this outcome?" If the answer is "less", change outcome #10 to something more important to you. If it's "more", then describe where in your body your feel this motivation? What sensations do you get, and where exactly, as you think about achieving each specific outcome?

Now take outcome #10, and write it down in this format (replace X with your outcome and Y with what it will do for you): "When I get to X, I would/will Y." Ask yourself: "And when I get Y, what will that do for me?". Write down your answers.

The question "what it will do for me?", gives you the key to unlock the deep hidden meanings of your seemingly earthly outcome. Ask sincerely and repeatedly, for outcome #10, what will the result do for you? And then ask again, what will THAT result do for you?

Take your original outcome #10, and quickly and without thinking, complete the following sentence: "Yes, BUT..."

We'll deal with these objections and obstacles later on, but in the meantime imagine each one of them as a huge rock blocking your path. Give each of them a specific color and a shape:

Take outcome #10 and rewrite it in a positive way. If you outcome is "to lose 10% body fat" or "eliminate my fear of flying", change it to something like, "my body has only 11% fat" and "I enjoy flying":

For outcome #10, answer: how will you know when you've achieved it? What exactly will happen then? What would you see, hear and feel, as this outcome becomes a reality? How would people behave around you? How will you behave around other people?

Think carefully about the context of your outcome #10. If your outcome is to be more passionate with your spouse, it would be only appropriate in certain locations and at certain times, not anywhere and anytime, right? For outcome #10, answer: Exactly when, where and with whom do you wish this outcome to be effective?

Consider the side effects of achieving outcome #10. Is there anything you or others will lose when you achieve this outcome? What are these things? Are you willing to accept the responsibility and consequences? How will you handle these losses?

Ask yourself: "Is achieving this outcome #10 within my control?"

For outcome #10 ask yourself, what skills and abilities and other resources (money, connections, knowledge, etc.) do you have currently, that make it more likely for you to achieve this outcome? Define the resources you will need to achieve outcome. Who can help you and how exactly? What physical items you absolutely need to make progress? What new skills you might have to learn? What information is needed and where will you get it? How much money is required? Be specific and thorough.

For outcome #10, specify: What do you still need to get or ask for, that you don't currently have, in order to achieve this outcome elegantly and promptly?

For outcome #10, specify: Who can help you get what you need to achieve your outcome? How else can you get anything else you need for the achievement of this outcome?

Build a mental representation of outcome #10. Is it possible for you to visualize the final result in your mind? Is it possible for you to see, hear, and feel what it will be like when you 'have it' in the near future? Write a paragraph or two describing this internal image for outcome #10.

Divide outcome #10 to 10 milestones. What are the most important action steps you must take in order to achieve this outcome within a realistic time frame?

1
2
3
4
5

6
7
8
9
10

Do you truly believe that pursuing outcome #10 is important and meaningful? If yes, why exactly? If not, why did you choose this outcome at all? (here you have a chance to rewrite it).

How exactly would you feel ashamed, guilty or anxious if you did less than your best to achieve outcome #10? Describe the inner conversation you will have with yourself if, a year or two from today, you regret not taking the appropriate action steps.

Do you want to achieve outcome #10 for personal reasons, or to please someone else? Is the pursuit of outcome #10 exciting? enjoyable? satisfying? Describe the feelings and sensations you're expecting from the journey towards fulfilling the outcome, from taking courageous actions and building your inner strength in the process.

Does outcome #10 represent a deeply felt personal dream? How would the disciplined and successful achievement of outcome #10 change the way that you see yourself?

How would achieving outcome #10 affect the lives of the people around you? Family, relatives, friends, colleagues? How would achieving outcome #10 affect the broader community you live in?

Until when exactly would you like to achieve outcome #10? Be specific. You can change the deadline later. How will you monitor your own behavior to ensure you're making progress towards your desired outcome #10?

How can you ensure you're not pushing yourself too hard and burning out while working on outcome #10? How would you know if the opposite is true - being too easy on yourself and becoming bored and cynical?

What is the first small step that you could take in the next 3 days, towards the realization of outcome #10? Write it down on a sticky note and attach it to your computer screen.

Action Steps Summary

1
2
3
4
5

6
7
8
9
10

Made in the USA
Las Vegas, NV
07 September 2022

54832723R00278